OXFORD
UNIVERSITY PRESS

CAMBRIDGE CHECKP✓INT AND BEYOND

ASPIRE
SUCCEED
PROGRESS

Complete English as a Second Language for Cambridge Secondary 1

Chris Akhurst, Lucy Bowley,
Clare Collinson, Lynette Simonis

Series editor: Rachel Beveridge

9

WORKBOOK

Oxford excellence for Cambridge Secondary 1

OXFORD

OXFORD
UNIVERSITY PRESS

Great Clarendon Street, Oxford, OX2 6DP, United Kingdom

Oxford University Press is a department of the University of Oxford. It furthers the University's objective of excellence in research, scholarship, and education by publishing worldwide. Oxford is a registered trade mark of Oxford University Press in the UK and in certain other countries

British Library Cataloguing in Publication Data
Data available

978-0-19-837817-4

10 9 8 7 6

Paper used in the production of this book is a natural, recyclable product made from wood grown in sustainable forests. The manufacturing process conforms to the environmental regulations of the country of origin.

Printed and bound by CPI Group (UK) Ltd, Croydon, CR0 4YY

Acknowledgements
The publishers would like to thank the following for permissions to use their photographs:

Cover: Glorious Havana, Wheatley, Jenny/Private Collection/Bridgeman Images

Artworks: Aptara, p67: Gustavo Berado

p74 (T): Rvector/Shutterstock; p74 (B): Rvector/Shutterstock; p75: MicroOne/Shutterstock; p79 (T): La Place Vendôme (oil on canvas), Cortes, Edouard Leon (1882-1969)/Private Collection/Photo © Christie's Images/Bridgeman Images; p79 (B): Dea Picture Library/Getty;

We are grateful to the authors and publishers for use of extracts from their titles and in particular for the following:

'Bee Hummingbirds: The Smallest Living Birds' from https://www.beautyofbirds.com/beehummingbirds.html. Reproduced by permission of Avianweb.

Extract from https://www.visitsealife.com/gweek. Reproduced by permission.

Although we have made every effort to trace and contact all copyright holders before publication this has not been possible in all cases. If notified, the publisher will rectify any errors or omissions at the earliest opportunity.

Contents

Humans and nature

1. What changes have people made in your town in recent years? Write down three changes which have been made, whether you think they are helpful or harmful changes, and why.

   For example: A new wildlife park was opened four years ago. This is a good change because it will provide protection for rare birds and animals.

   a ....

   ....

   ....

   b ....

   ....

   c ....

   ....

2. There might be several changes your town could make to help nature. Write down one change you would like to see happen that would help nature. Why would you like this to happen?

   For example: I would like to see more flowers in the park, not just grass and trees. I would like this to happen because flowers attract all kinds of insects, and I like learning about insects.

   ....

   ....

   ....

3. Why is it important for people to think about the nature which surrounds them? Why do we sometimes have to help nature? Write two sentences to give your opinion.

   ....

   ....

   ....

   ....

Cornish Seal Sanctuary, Gweek

Cornwall is an area in the south west of the United Kingdom (UK) which is popular with tourists. Read the following website extracts which provide information about the Cornish Seal Sanctuary in the village of Gweek.

At the **Cornish** Seal **Sanctuary**, we have lots of local activities you can support or get involved with!

We work hard to protect every part of our oceans and the sea life that lives within it. Whether the **threat** is man-made, due to population changes in the wild, or an effect of **global warming**, we take action....

The Cornish Seal Sanctuary ... **annually** rescues, cares for and returns to the wild more than 100 **orphaned**, injured and sick seal pups ...

... We also have some very playful **residents** including Grey Seals, Common Seals, Californian Sea Lions, Patagonian Sea Lions, Otters, Penguins ... that live with us at the Cornish Seal Sanctuary Gweek....

... Come and meet our residents, enjoy our wide open spaces and enjoy a relaxing drink or snack in our Seal Sanctuary Cafe.

Glossary

annually each year

Cornish comes from Cornwall, a county in the UK

global warming the heating up of the planet because of pollution

orphaned without parents

residents people or animals who live in a particular place

sanctuary a safe place

threat the possibility of trouble or danger

Now answer these questions about the extracts above.

1. Give two reasons a seal pup might be at the seal sanctuary.

....

....

2. Give two examples of things you can do at the sanctuary, other than looking at seals.

....

....

3. Which of these is not found at the sanctuary? (Circle more than one.)

| penguin | otter | sea lion | whale | pelican |

4. How does the sanctuary help the environment? Give one example.

....

5. Which animal at Gweek would you be most interested in learning more about and why?

....

Nouns

Fill the gaps in the following sentences with abstract nouns made from the words in brackets. You can use a dictionary to help you if you wish.

1. The sanctuary provides .... and .... for injured seals. (protect/secure)

2. The manager thanked the staff for their .... and .... (commit/assist)

3. We heard an interesting .... about the .... projects the sanctuary is involved in. (present/conserve)

4. Do you think it is our .... to help animals that are harmed by ....? (responsible/pollute)

Make compound nouns by adding the words from the box to the words below.

back	post	change	time
line	seller	confidence	warming

5. global ....
6. head ....
7. climate ....
8. day ....
9. feed ....
10. self- ....
11. sign ....
12. best ....

Underline all the countable nouns and circle all the uncountable nouns in the following sentences.

13. The sanctuary is located in beautiful countryside near the coast.

14. I was enjoying my walk in the sunshine when I saw a seal on the sand.

15. There are no clouds in the sky today, although the forecast predicted rain.

16. Pollution can affect the quality of the air we breathe and the water we drink.

17. She has patience and determination, which are important qualities in her job.

18. Many people who love nature visit this area to see the wildlife and spectacular scenery.

 Remember

Many abstract nouns end in a suffix. *Examples*: pay**ment**, prepar**ation**, conclu**sion**, attrac**tion**, differ**ence**, guid**ance**, ill**ness**, activ**ity**

Remember

Compound nouns are made up of two or more words. *Examples*: wildlife, full moon, great-grandmother

Remember

- Most uncountable nouns do not have a plural form.
- Some nouns can be countable and uncountable, depending on how they are used.

Forestry Commission

 <u>Track 1.1</u> The Forestry Commission is an organisation which looks after forests all over the UK. It protects them for the future and educates people about forests. Listen to Nick giving a talk about his work with the Forestry Commission and then answer the questions that follow.

For each question, circle the correct answer A, B or C.

1. How long has Nick worked at the Forestry Commission?

   A 20 years   **B** nearly 20 years   **C** over 20 years

2. Nick says the most important part of the work the Forestry Commission does is:

   A planting trees   **B** buying land   **C** going into schools

Write answers to these questions.

3. What did Nick do immediately after finishing university, and why?

   ....

   ....

4. Give two details about Nick's work for the Forestry Commission.

   ....

   ....

> ## Glossary
> **forestry** looking after forests
> **fungi** living things like mushrooms that can grow on a tree
> **insight** a deep understanding

5. Which part of the Forestry Commission's work interests you the most, and why?

   ....

   ....

6. There is not just one type of tree – there are thousands of different kinds around the world. Do some research on the Internet or in your local library and find out the names of five more types of tree to add to the list below:

   a ....oak........   **b** ......cedar......   **c** ....   **d** ....

   e ....   **f** ....   **g** ....

7. People can use different types of wood to make different objects. Pick two of the types of tree you named in question 6 and then find out how the wood from these trees can be used by humans.

   For example: Oak is often used to make heavy furniture. Cedar is often used to make pencils.

   ....

   ....

Determiners and quantifiers

Fill the gaps in the following sentences with determiners from the box.

any	what	this	other

1. Look at .... fruit tree. It is covered in apples.

2. Do you know .... kind of tree this is?

3. He reminded visitors that they shouldn't leave .... rubbish behind.

4. Nick said he learned a lot about trees by visiting .... countries.

For each gap in the following paragraph, circle the most suitable word or phrase from the list below.

Almost …(5)… the Earth's land surface is covered by forest. Forests provide food and shelter for …(6)… kinds of wildlife, including …(7)… the world's most endangered animals. Like …(8)… green plants, trees produce a gas called oxygen, which humans and …(9)… animals need to live. However, …(10)… year, …(11)… of trees are cut down and in …(12)… parts of the world large …(13)… forest have been completely destroyed. This can cause …(14)… damage to the environment. Areas that are left with …(15)… trees are at greater risk of flooding. When trees are cut down, we need to plant …(16)… young trees to replace them.

5.	a third	a third of	third
6.	much	many	many of
7.	some of	some	several
8.	every	each	all
9.	other	another	every
10.	all	every	either
11.	millions of	millions	a million
12.	some	each	any
13.	areas of	numbers of	items of
14.	many	several	much
15.	less	fewer	little
16.	enough	much	a great deal of

> **Remember**
>
> A determiner is a word that comes at the beginning of a noun phrase. *Examples:* a/an, the, this, any, another, other, my, her, their, which, what, whose

> **Remember**
>
> - Quantifiers are determiners that tell us how many or how much there is of something. *Examples:* all, few, several, lots of, more, most, enough, no
> - We often use quantifiers followed by 'of' and another determiner. *Example:* some of his ideas

> **Remember**
>
> To say how much there is of an uncountable noun, we often use phrases such as 'a piece of', 'a packet of' and 'a slice of'.

Nature project

From: Team leader

To: All team members

Subject: Help needed

The Oldtown nature project was started with the hope of providing a realistic environment for local wildlife such as owls and **hedgehogs**, both of which are **nocturnal**. Over the past year, however, rats are the only kind of wildlife which have been attracted to the area.

I need a member of the team to review the project to advise how it can be made better.

Many thanks,

Shona

Read Shona's email to her team. You are part of Shona's team and have been asked to research how to attract more owls and hedgehogs to the area. You will present your findings to the team. Use the questions below to help you prepare your presentation.

> **Glossary**
>
> **hedgehog** a small, brown animal with sharp spines on its back
>
> **nocturnal** awake at night

1. Are there any words in the email you don't understand? Check their meaning in a dictionary, and try to use them correctly in your presentation.

2. You need to find out more about the wildlife you wish to attract. Use the following questions to help with your research:
   - What do owls and hedgehogs need in their environment?
   - What are their homes like?
   - When are they active and looking for food?
   - What do they eat?

3. Decide what needs to happen to make the area more attractive to owls and hedgehogs. Write down three ideas for your plan.

Now in your notebook, write notes for your presentation. Practise it out loud to yourself and then, if possible, say it to a friend or family member. They can ask you questions afterwards.

Giving nature a helping hand

You have received the following information about the Premium Project, a project which helps nature.

The **Premium** Project was set up four years ago to help communities use and **preserve** the nature around them.

For example, if the local community wants to create a garden, the Premium Project donates flowers which attract butterflies and bees to the area and this also makes sure local crops do well. The new gardens also benefit **the elderly**, giving them somewhere to visit and making them happier citizens.

Finally, schoolchildren visit the Premium Project gardens each week to learn about how important plants are for our futures.

Now you are going to write an email to tell a friend about the Premium Project. Include:

- three facts that you want to tell them about the Premium Project
- why they would enjoy building a new garden in their community and why they would be good at it
- one example of a new skill they would learn from the experience and why this would be a good skill to have.

Now write your email to your friend, remembering to use informal language.

Write 80–100 words.

Glossary

premium of high quality or value

preserve to prevent something from being damaged or destroyed

the elderly people who are old

Quiz

1. Write down one idea you have to help wildlife in your local area.

....

2. Why is it important for people to help nature? Give one reason.

....

3. Give two examples of animals other than seals which live at the Cornish Seal Sanctuary.

....

....

4. Which four of the following nouns can be both countable and uncountable, depending on how they are used? Circle the correct answers.

gas	hedgehog	wildlife
wood	tree	leaf
conservation	glass	stone

5. In Track 1.1, what does Nick say he learned about when he lived abroad? (Listen to the recording again if you need to.)

....

....

6. According to Track 1.1, decide if the following statement is true or false.
'All fungi harm trees'.

a true   **b** false

7. Fill the gaps in the following sentences with the most suitable determiner or quantifier from the brackets.

a .... of the trees in this forest have a disease. (A few/A little)

b We mustn't chop down .... of these two trees. (neither/either)

c Don't leave .... rubbish behind in the forest. (some/any)

8. Which word can be used to describe the fact that owls are awake at night?

....

Record breakers

1. Why do people want to break a world record? Add your own ideas to the list below:

   Feeling of achievement, money, ...

   ....

2. If you were trying to break a world record, what would you say to inspire yourself? Write down your own saying that you can look at when you need a bit of motivation.

   ....

   ....

3. Imagine you met someone who had broken a world record. Write down three words you could use to describe them.

   ....

4. When people try to break a world record, there are many things that can make the difference between success and failure. These might include the weather, possible dangers, help from other people (if permitted) and access to training and equipment.

   Look at the following examples and write down one thing you would include in the plans for each record **attempt** to help make it a success.

   a The longest solo journey by **canoe**. ....

   ....

   b The highest **skydive** without a **parachute**. ....

   ....

   c The longest pizza ever. ....

   ....

   d The most countries visited in 24 hours. ....

   ....

Glossary

attempt when you try to do something

canoe a long narrow boat

parachute large piece of material that helps a person to land safely

skydive jumping from an aeroplane

Records in nature: The bee hummingbird

Read this short fact file about the world's smallest bird, the bee hummingbird, and then answer the questions.

The bee hummingbird...is a tiny bird that is only found in Cuba – a Caribbean island south of Florida, USA – and possibly on nearby islands.

Bee hummingbirds are the smallest known living birds in the world – being **comparable** in size to **bumble bees** – and are lighter than a Canadian or US penny [coin]. Females are slightly larger than males.

They **measure** mostly...5–6 cm in length – including **beak** and tail; and they weigh 1.6–1.9 g.

They **primarily** feed on **nectar** taken from a variety of brightly coloured, **scented** small flowers...visiting up to 1,500 flowers on an average day.

Glossary

beak the hard outside part of a bird's mouth

bumble bee a larger type of bee

comparable similar

measure to check the size, weight or height of something

nectar a type of sugar found in flowers

scented having a (usually) nice smell

primarily most of the time

Now answer these questions.

1. On which island is the bee hummingbird definitely found? ....

2. What is its longest length? ....

3. What is the usual maximum weight of a bee hummingbird? ....

4. What do bee hummingbirds eat? ....

5. How many flowers does a bee hummingbird visit each day? ....

6. Write down two world record facts about animals that you would like to know, then research and write down the answers. For example: I would like to know which animal is the fastest on land. / The fastest animal on land is the cheetah.

....

....

....

....

Adjectives

Fill the gaps in the following sentences with an adjective ending in –ing or –ed made from the verb in brackets.

1. She felt a bit .... because she didn't break the record. (disappoint)

2. We faced a .... climb to the top of the mountain. (challenge)

3. I was .... to learn that such a small bird visits so many flowers. (astonish)

Answer this question.

4. Use the words in the box to complete the compound adjectives in the following paragraph.

> | land | cup | pea | red | green |

> Bee hummingbirds mainly feed on wood...........................
> flowers in Cuba. At certain times of the year, the male
> has a fiery-........................... head and throat, with
> bluish-........................... feathers on the upper part of its
> body. The females build tiny, ...-shaped
> homes in which they lay two ....-sized
> eggs.

Fill the gaps in the following sentences with a suitable adverb.

5. The bee hummingbird is .... small and its feathers are .... stunning.

6. The bird is not only .... special, it is also .... unique.

Fill the gaps in the following sentences with the correct comparative or superlative form of the adjective in brackets.

7. The female bee hummingbird is a bit .... than the male. (large)

8. It is easily the .... bird I have ever seen. (beautiful)

9. Bee hummingbirds used to be much .... than they are now. (common)

Remember

- Adjectives that end in –ed often describe feelings. Adjectives ending in –ing often describe the cause of the feelings.

- We often use compound adjectives to describe someone's character, or the appearance of something or someone.

Remember

- We use adverbs such as 'very', 'extremely' and 'quite' to make most adjectives stronger. To make extreme adjectives stronger, we use adverbs such as 'absolutely', 'totally' and 'completely'.

- To make comparative adjectives stronger, we use words such as 'far', 'much', 'a bit' or 'slightly'. To make superlative adjectives stronger, we use words such as 'by far' and 'easily'.

Welcome to MegaLand

 **Track 2.1** Listen to Simon Khan, the park manager of MegaLand, one of the world's newest and largest theme parks.

For each of these questions, circle the correct answer A, B or C.

1. How many people work at the park?

   A 150   **B** 1,500   **C** 15,000

2. How many different types of food can you eat in the theme park?

   A 13   **B** 30   **C** 33

Write the answers to these questions.

3. How does the park check where people are? ....

....

4. What will happen if there are too many people in one area? ....

....

5. How can people remember their visit to the park? ....

....

 **Track 2.2** Now listen to a tour guide talking about the facts and figures of the park. Complete the notes below as you listen.

Final cost to build MegaLand: _____

_____

When building started: _____

_____

Number of zones in the park now: _____

_____

Number of languages spoken by

staff members: _____

_____

Number of world records MegaLand

hopes to have by 2019: _____

_____

Adverbs

Fill the gaps in the following sentences with an adverb from the box.

> every day   safely   really   luckily

1. ...., we were the first in the queue.

2. The staff make sure visitors move around the park ....

3. Everyone had a .... good time.

4. Thousands of people visit the park ....

For each sentence, choose the correct meaning, A or B.

5. Only children can go on this ride.

   A No adults can go on this ride.

   B This is the only ride children can go on.

6. Everyone had a good time, especially Jo and Ana.

   A Jo and Ana enjoyed themselves slightly more than the others.

   B Jo and Ana didn't have a very good time.

7. Sara didn't particularly enjoy the rides.

   A Sara quite enjoyed the rides.

   B Sara didn't enjoy the rides very much.

8. Our journey took exactly two hours.

   A Our journey took almost two hours.

   B Our journey took two hours.

Select the correct adverb to complete the following sentences.

9. The adults enjoyed themselves just as .... as the children.

   A more   **B** most   **C** much

10. We found our way around the park far .... than we were expecting.

    A more easily   **B** easily   **C** easiest

11. We had all come a long way, but Jo had come the ....

    A furthest   **B** further   **C** most far

Remember

- Adverbs of **manner** (how) usually come after the main verb or after the object if there is one.
- Adverbs of **time** (when) often come at the end of a clause or sentence.
- Adverbs of **degree** (amount) usually come before the verb, adjective or adverb they modify.
- **Sentence** adverbs, such as 'unfortunately', often come at the start of a sentence.

Remember

Some adverbs, such as 'only', 'just', 'particularly' and 'especially', focus attention on a particular action, thing or part of a sentence.

Remember

- We use comparative adverbs + 'than' to compare two actions. We use superlative adverbs to compare the actions of more than two people or things.
- We can make comparisons using words and phrases such as '(not) as … as' and 'just as … as', 'far', 'a lot', 'a bit' and 'slightly'.

Interview with a reporter

Your class has completed its world record attempt for the longest group dance and you are now being interviewed by a local reporter. Answer the reporter's questions, and also include what you think the reporter might say at the end of the interview.

WORLD RECORD

Reporter: You and your class have just become world record holders. How do you feel?

You: ....

....

Reporter: How did you prepare for today?

You: ....

....

Reporter: What is the secret of your success?

You: ....

....

Reporter: What made you sure it could be done?

You: ....

....

Reporter: Who has helped you do this today?

You: ....

Reporter: What would you like to say to your supporters and the spectators here?

You: ....

....

Reporter: What will you do next?

You: ....

Reporter: ....

....

....

When you have decided what you are going to say, practise reading it aloud. Think about your pronunciation. If you can, ask a friend or family member to take the role of the reporter.

Writing an email

You are going to write an email to your favourite celebrity about another world record attempt that your class will be doing. First, choose another group world record that you have either discussed in class or read about, then think about the 'who', 'why', 'what', 'where', 'when' and 'how' of your record attempt, including the following:

- What three things will your group have to do before they can break the record? For example, they might need to do some training. Try to be as specific as you can.

- How many of you will be making the attempt and what will your roles be?

- Why are you making this record attempt? Try to think of two reasons to include in your email.

Now write a short email to your chosen celebrity, asking them for some words of support and advice before you start your world record attempt. Remember to introduce yourself and use the correct words to end your email.

Write 80–120 words.

....

....

....

....

....

....

....

....

....

....

....

Quiz

1. Write down three adjectives to describe a world record breaker.

....

2. Rewrite the following sentences, correcting the mistakes.

a The rollercoaster was by far the better ride in the park.

....

b The female hummingbird is slightly bigger the male.

....

c The bird is as small than a bee.

....

3. Write down the name of one of the fastest animals in the world.

....

4. Fill the gaps in the following sentences with an adverb from the box.

> sadly   especially   absolutely   just

a We had an .... amazing day at the park.
b We felt a bit bored, ... when we were waiting in the queue.
c ...., the park is closing so we have to leave.
d We arrived at the park .... before it closed.

5. Write down one sentence to motivate someone who wants to break a world record.

....

6. Write down two words to describe how you would feel if you broke a world record.

....

7. Give one reason why someone might not succeed in breaking a world record.

....

8. How could the example of a world record breaker change our daily lives to achieve the best results we can?

....

....

....

3 Unusual careers

I would prefer an unusual career because:

- it would make my life more varied and exciting

- it would make me more interesting to other people

- I want to do something that I never grow tired of.

1. Can you add two more reasons why someone might prefer an unusual job?

....

....

2. Unusual jobs could be described as 'exciting', 'different' and 'challenging'. Add two more adjectives to describe an unusual job.

....

3. Some people prefer to work in the same job or organisation for their whole career and might not want a new or unusual job.

> I prefer to know what will happen at work, with no surprises.

> I like to be able to come home at the same time each night.

Can you add one more reason?

....

4. Are you more likely to want an unusual job or an ordinary job? Choose a job that interests you and then write down three reasons for your choice.

....

....

....

The beekeeper

Read about Sammy the beekeeper and then answer the questions that follow.

Sammy first became interested in bees about ten years ago when he saw a news story about the falling numbers of honey bees around the world. The reporter said that if nothing was done, the number of bees would fall even further and they could soon become **extinct**.

So Sammy decided to go to his local **beekeeping** club to ask for more information. Four other people who had seen the news story also turned up that evening. The beekeeping club was very pleased and decided to give a free **hive** and a **queen bee** to each person who had turned up, and gave them instructions on how to keep bees. Sammy collected his hive and his bee, which he placed in his garden.

Ten years later, Sammy now owns 200 hives in various locations within 80 kilometres of his home. He makes around 6,000 jars of honey each year, which he sells to a national supermarket chain.

Glossary

beekeeping owning and looking after bees and collecting their honey

extinct no longer existing

hive a wooden box where bees live

queen bee the most important bee in the hive

For each question circle the correct answer A, B or C.

1. What made Sammy become interested in bees?

   A to collect honey   **B** to help save the bee population   **C** to make money

2. Why did Sammy go to the local beekeeping club?

   A to tell them the news   **B** to ask for information   **C** to ask for honey

Write answers to these questions.

3. What did the beekeeping club give Sammy?

   ....

4. What does Sammy do with the jars of honey he makes?

   ....

5. You would like your school to have its own hive of bees. How are you going to persuade the head teacher to have one? Write down three reasons why your school should have a hive.

   ....

   ....

   ....

Prepositions

Underline the prepositional phrase in each of the following sentences.

1. Sammy has kept bees for ten years.

2. He makes money by selling honey.

3. This is the hive with the new queen bee.

Fill the gaps in the following sentences with a suitable preposition.

4. .... first, he just had one hive.

5. This is .... far the best job I've had.

6. Thanks .... bees, we can eat honey.

For each gap in the following paragraph, circle the most suitable preposition in the list below.

I got …(7)… my career …(8)… chance when I became concerned …(9)… the falling number of bees. I started …(10)… keeping a hive …(11)… fun. It was different …(12)… anything else I'd done. Then, …(13)… receiving lots of advice …(14)… how to run a business, I made beekeeping my career. …(15)… my point of view, beekeeping is the perfect job. I enjoy working …(16)… my own and looking …(17)… the bees …(18)… the fresh air. I am surprised …(19)… how well the business is doing, but I am very proud …(20)… the honey.

7.	in	into	14. to	on
8.	by	for	15. From	For
9.	about	for	16. for	on
10.	for	by	17. for	after
11.	with	for	18. in	with
12.	from	as	19. at	for
13.	after	by	20. with	of

Remember

- A prepositional phrase starts with a preposition and ends with a noun, pronoun, noun phrase or gerund. *Examples:* at work, with them, to his local club, by listening
- We often use prepositions before nouns and adjectives in common prepositional phrases. *Examples:* for example, out of work, on the whole, in general

Remember

We often use prepositions after nouns, adjectives and verbs. *Examples:* reason for, famous for, prepare for

Career focus: Tennis racket stringer

<u>Track 3.1</u> In the recording you will hear Johan talk about his job. He travels the world with the top tennis players and is there to string their rackets for when the players need them. Listen to Johan talk about his job.

Glossary

on the road travelling a long way or often

strung having strings attached and arranged

tension being stretched tight

For each of these questions, circle the correct answer A, B or C.

1. In which season did Johan attend the racket-stringing course?

   A spring   **B** summer   **C** autumn

2. Why did Johan originally want to learn about racket stringing?

   A to get a new job

   B to meet tennis professionals

   C to improve as a tennis player

3. How often do tennis professionals have their rackets checked to make sure the tension is correct?

   A between matches   **B** between tournaments   **C** between seasons

Write answers to these questions.

4. Which three parts of the body could be injured if a racket is strung too tightly?

   ....

5. In which month does the tennis season start? ....

6. Which city is Johan's favourite? ....

7. What do you think is the best part of Johan's job? Write an email to a friend telling them about Johan and give them one reason why you especially like his job.

   Write 60–80 words. Remember you are writing to a friend, so you need to use informal language.

   ....

   ....

   ....

   ....

   ....

   ....

   ....

Pronouns and relative clauses

For each gap in the following sentences circle the correct pronoun.

1. Before the course, I didn't know *much/many* about the tension of strings.

2. *Anybody/Everybody* is very friendly at the tournaments.

3. I strung the racket *myself/himself*, so I knew the tension would be correct.

4. We had been travelling a lot, so we decided to give *us/ourselves* a break.

5. I wanted to find out how to string rackets. *Those/That* is why I went on the course.

Fill the gaps in the following sentences with a suitable relative pronoun. More than one answer may be possible.

6. The tennis player .... I was speaking to was very friendly.

7. Even the famous players are supportive, ... I wasn't expecting.

8. This racket, ... is made of wood, was given to me by a friend.

9. The strings in this racket are too loose, ... makes it hard to use.

10. New York is the city .... he likes most.

Answer these questions.

11. In which two sentences in questions 6–10 can the relative pronouns be left out?

   ....

12. Which two sentences in questions 6–10 include relative clauses that refer to a whole clause?

   ....

> **Remember**
>
> We use:
> - **demonstrative pronouns** (this, these, that, those) to refer to particular people or things, and things that we have already talked about
> - **indefinite pronouns** (somebody, anything, etc.) to refer to people and things less specifically
> - **reflexive pronouns** (myself, herself, etc.) when the subject and object of a verb are the same, to emphasise a person or thing and after some verbs that have two objects
> - pronouns such as 'much', 'some' and 'any' to talk about **quantities**
> - **relative pronouns** (who, which, that, etc.) to introduce relative clauses.

> **Remember**
>
> - Relative clauses sometimes refer to a whole clause. *Example:* My racket is broken, **which is annoying**.
> - When a relative pronoun is the object of the clause, we can leave it out. *Example:* Has he mended the racket (that) I lent you?

Employee wanted (job includes travel)

1. You are in charge of a company that requires its employees to travel around the world, often on their own and with little warning of where they will have to go or for how long. What three questions would you ask in an interview for a new employee?

   For example: How would you feel about spending a lot of time on aeroplanes?

   ....

   ....

   ....

2. In the interview one person looks suitable for the job but is not sure about the travelling that is required. Write down three benefits of travel which might make them change their mind.

   For example: If you travel, you can learn new languages.

   ....

   ....

   ....

3. Complete the following script with your interviewer questions. Then write the answers that you would give if you were applying for this job. Also include what the interviewer might say at the end of the interview.

   Interviewer: How would you feel about spending a lot of time on aeroplanes?

   You: ....

   Interviewer: ....

   You: ....

   Interviewer: ....

   You: ....

   Interviewer: ....

   You: ....

   Interviewer: ....

   Now practise your pronunciation by reading the script aloud to yourself, or practise it with a friend or family member if possible.

Make an 'ordinary' job more unusual

You are going to write a short story about someone with an 'ordinary' job who goes to work one day and discovers that their job has suddenly become very unusual.

Start by imagining the most ordinary job you can think of, and then think about the following questions.

- What is the title of the job and where is the job located?

- What three things about the job make it seem 'ordinary' to you?

- How could these three things be changed to make them more unusual?

- Who is your main character, and how are they going to respond to the changes?

Now write your story. You may want to start the story at the beginning of the day when the main character arrives at work, or later when they are telling a friend about the unusual day they have just had. Write 100–150 words.

....

....

....

....

....

....

....

....

....

....

....

....

....

Quiz

1. Write one sentence to explain why Sammy enjoys being a beekeeper.

....

....

2. Write two adjectives to describe an unusual job of your choice. Then write sentences using each of those adjectives.

....

....

....

3. Fill the gaps in the following sentences with a suitable preposition.

a I saw an advertisement .... an interesting job.

b Sammy became interested .... bees about ten years ago.

c He cares a lot .... the environment.

4. What is the name given to the wooden house where bees often live? Circle the correct answer A, B or C.

A a home

B a hive

C a beekeeper

5. Write down one advantage of being a tennis racket stringer.

....

6. Write one advantage of choosing to do an unusual job.

....

7. Write down two examples of jobs that exist now but did not exist in the past.

....

....

8. Fill the gaps in the following sentences with a suitable pronoun.

a My job involves a lot of travelling, ... is why I enjoy it.

b His business, ... he started ten years ago, is very successful.

c She makes all the travel arrangements ....

Famous buildings

You have been asked to redecorate a local community centre with a group of friends. Remember it is used by lots of different people of different ages so the design must be suitable for everybody.

Design a plan for redecorating the community centre and write a description of the plan in the form below.

<u>Redecoration project details</u>

1. What does the building look like and why does it need changing?

....

....

....

2. What are your plans, and what will the new building look like?

....

....

....

3. What materials will be required? (For example: paint.)

....

....

4. What will the building be used for?

....

....

....

5. How will the new decoration improve the community centre?

....

....

....

....

Awesome architecture

Dubai is known for its spectacular buildings, but did you know that there are plans for the **construction** of the following buildings?

First, plans for a 'Technosphere' have been put forward by a company that has already won many architectural awards for its innovative designs. The Technosphere will be a unique building in terms of its shape and size. The 64-storey design is based on the shape of planet Earth and the outside will consist of glass and **solar panels**.

Next there is the 'Floating Seahorse **villas**' project. Property developers have designed **luxury** villas with three storeys, one of which is underwater. The idea is that people can sleep under the sea, with underwater life all around them.

Finally, 'Rosemont Hotel and **Residences**' will be a **skyscraper** including 448 hotel rooms and 280 **serviced** apartments, and a 7,000-square-metre tropical rainforest! There will be waterfalls, streams, a **sandless** beach and adventure trails. With this project, the architects plan to transform a 'typical hotel stay' into something very different.

For each of these questions, circle the correct answer A, B or C.

1. What is the Technosphere's design based on?

    A a football   **B** a sphere   **C** planet Earth

2. What is special about 'Floating Seahorse villas'?

    A Part of the villa is underwater.

    B All of the villa is underwater.

    C The garden of the villa is underwater.

Write answers to these questions.

3. Which of the buildings will not be as tall as the others?

4. For each of the spectacular building designs, write one sentence briefly describing the main details.

    The Technosphere: ....

    ....

    Floating Seahorse villas: ....

    ....

    Rosemont Hotel and Residences: ....

    ....

Glossary

construction making

luxury expensive, pleasant and comfortable

residences places where people live, such as houses

sandless without sand

serviced supplied with furniture and regularly cleaned

skyscraper a very tall building

solar panels sheets to collect sunlight to turn it into electricity

villas large and/or expensive houses

Active, passive and causative forms

Fill the gaps in the sentences below with present simple or past simple passive forms of the verbs in brackets.

1. Dubai .... for its impressive buildings. (know)

2. The building plans .... last month. (submit)

3. Building work .... often .... by the weather. (affect)

4. Yesterday, this room .... for a conference. (reserve)

Rewrite the following sentences as active sentences. Use the words in brackets as the subject of the sentences.

5. The apartments are cleaned regularly. (the staff)

....

6. The old theatre was knocked down. (the builders)

....

7. This building is often used for meetings. (people)

....

Complete the second sentence so that it has a similar meaning to the first, using the causative form 'have/get something done'. The first one has been done for you.

8. Our house was painted last year.

We had our house painted last year.

9. Their solar panels were installed yesterday.

They..

....

10. The manager's keys were stolen this morning.

The manager ....

....

11. The architects' original design was rejected.

The architects ....

12. One of their windows was replaced.

They ....

Radio special: Famous architects

 <u>Track 4.1</u> You are going to listen to a children's radio broadcast on famous architects. As you listen, make notes on the architects and then answer the following questions.

For each of these questions, circle the correct answer A, B or C.

1. What has Francine Houben said about architecture?

   A it must appeal to all of a person's senses

   B it must be beautiful

   C it must be noticeable

2. What inspired Antoni Gaudí's designs?

   A the city   **B** other buildings   **C** nature

3. Why is the Burj Al Arab in Dubai one of the most recognisable buildings in the world?

   A It is the world's tallest building.

   B It looks like a ship's sail.

   C It looks like a bridge.

4. Where is the White House?

   A New York   **B** Washington, D.C.   **C** Baltimore

5. Gustave Eiffel was known as which of the following?

   A a mechanic   **B** a bridge builder and engineer   **C** an artist

6. What do all the architects in the radio programme have in common?

   A They have all designed famous buildings.

   B They have all used the same building materials.

   C They have all designed buildings using the same vision.

Write an answer to this question.

7. Which of the buildings or architects do you find most interesting? Give reasons for your choice.

....

....

....

Present and past continuous

Circle the correct verb form, A, B or C, to fill the gaps in the following sentences.

1. .... on holiday next year?

   A Do you go   **B** Are you going   **C** Were you going

2. We .... with some friends in Paris when I went up the Eiffel Tower.

   A are staying   **B** staying   **C** were staying

3. The tour guide .... the tickets when I arrived.

   A is handing out   **B** was handing out   **C** handing out

4. I .... Gaudí's buildings to be so colourful.

   A am not expecting   **B** was expecting   **C** wasn't expecting

Answer this question.

5. **Use present continuous active or passive forms of the verbs in the word box to complete the following conversation.**

hope	fit	live	move back	rent	decorate

Jacinta: Where .... you .... at the moment?

Mara: We .... an apartment on the edge of town. Our house .... The builders .... the new heating system this week.

Jacinta: .... you .... again after that?

Mara: Yes, we .... to be back home soon.

Rewrite the following sentences in the past continuous, active or passive.

6. The population of the town increased.

   ....

7. Some new apartments were built.

   ....

8. The roof always leaks.

   ....

9. Did they build a new hospital?

   ....

Remember

We make the **present continuous** with a present form of 'be' (am/is/are) + a present participle (–ing). To make the **past continuous**, we use a past form of 'be' (was/were) + a present participle. *Example:* They **are/were building** our house.

Remember

- To make passive forms, we use a present or past form of 'be' + 'being' + past participle. *Example:* My house **is/was being built**.

- In questions, we put the auxiliary (am/is/are/was/were, etc.) before the subject. *Example:* What **are you** doing?

Research an architect

Using the Internet or your shool library, do some research to find an architect you haven't heard of before. Make notes on the architect and one of their famous buildings, and then practise speaking about them. Your talk should be about two minutes long.

Use the following questions to help you with your research.

- Which architect and famous building will you choose?
- What facts and information can you include on the architect and building?
- What does the building represent?
- What else is the architect known for?
- Are there any pictures that you could use as part of your talk?

Write notes to help you remember the important facts and information about your new architect.

> ## Remember
>
> Think of ways to make your talk more interesting. You could include:
>
> - rhetorical questions – 'Did you know . . .?'
> - direct address – 'you'
> - pictures of the building
> - examples of other buildings designed by the architect.

....

....

....

....

....

....

....

....

....

....

....

If you can, share your talk on your architect with a friend or family member. They can ask you questions about the architect you chose to speak about.

Writing an online travel blog

You are going to write an online travel blog about a famous building. Remember, you need to describe the building but you also need to encourage people to go and visit it. Choose from one of the following:

The Eiffel Tower, Paris

The Acropolis, Athens

The Empire State Building, New York

The Forbidden City, China

The Colosseum, Rome

The Sydney Opera House

The Leaning Tower of Pisa

Taj Majal, India

Think about the layout of your blog. Use the following checklist as a guide, and tick to show you have included each of these:

☐ Title

☐ Subheading

☐ Facts and statistics

☐ Information about the building and architect

☐ Descriptive words

Quiz

1. What is a redecoration project? Circle the correct answer A, B or C.

   A when you change the appearance of the inside of a building

   B when you create a new building

   C when you knock down an old building

2. Match each word below to its correct meaning.

   a villa   a very tall building

   b residence   a large or expensive building

   c skyscraper   a place where someone lives

3. Circle the sentence that includes an **incorrect** passive or causative form.

   A The meeting was postponed.

   B We are having the building materials delivered on Friday.

   C The hotel is having its floors cleaned yesterday.

4. Which is likely to be the opinion of Francine Houben? Circle the correct answer A, B or C.

   A Architecture is about the beauty of the building.

   B Architecture is about the people, place and purpose.

   C Architecture is about curves and lines.

5. What is Antoni Gaudí famous for? Circle the correct answer A, B or C.

   A grey and white colours, curves and use of light

   B straight lines, interesting materials and use of light

   C curves, bright colours and interesting materials

6. Put the words in the correct order to make sentences.

   a next/visiting/Barcelona/we/are/week

      ....

   b some/built/are/apartments/new/being/there

      ....

   c saw/being/fitted/the house/I/the windows/when/were

      ....

7. What makes famous buildings special in your opinion?

   ....

8. Is it important for architects to design buildings that amaze us? Give a reason for your answer.

   ....

⑤ On your own

1. How would you describe being on your own? Complete the two lists below, adding positive words and phrases to the first list and negative words and phrases to the second list.

   Positive

   an opportunity to think things through

   a challenge

   ....

   ....

   ....

   Negative

   frightening
   very uncomfortable

   ....

   ....

   ....

2. Write two short descriptions of times when you were alone, the first when you felt frightened and the second when you enjoyed it. Try to use some of the words and phrases from your lists above.

   Feeling frightened

   ....

   ....

   ....

   An enjoyable time

   ....

   ....

   ....

Rainforest survivor

Read how a teenager from Peru survived alone in the wild and answer the questions that follow.

On 24 December 1971, seventeen-year-old Juliane Koepcke was on her way to join her father in Pucallpa, eastern Peru, when the plane she was in was struck by lightning and crashed. Amazingly, she **survived** with only a broken **collarbone** and a few cuts and **bruises**, but she found herself alone, deep in thick rainforest.

She found some sweets among what was left of the plane and these were all she had to eat for nine days. During this time she carefully followed the survival rules that her father, a **biologist**, had taught her. She discovered a small stream, which provided her with drinking water, and treated her **injuries** and the many insect bites she received in ways she had learned from her father. By floating **downstream** she eventually came to a hut and was rescued.

Glossary

biologist a scientist who studies biology

bruises dark areas on skin hurt from a knock or a fall

collarbone the bone between neck and shoulder

downstream further down the stream, in the direction the water flows

injuries parts of the body that have been damaged

survived did not die

For each question circle the correct answer A, B or C.

1. Where was Juliane travelling to when the plane crashed?

   A eastern Peru   **B** western Peru   **C** a thick rainforest

2. Who had taught her how to survive alone?

   A she taught herself   **B** her father   **C** her biology teacher

3. What did she drink?

   A rainwater   **B** water from a stream   **C** nothing – she just ate sweets

Write answers to these questions.

4. Explain in your own words the advice that Juliane had been given about how to survive.

   ....

   ....

5. Continue the following blog or email to a friend:

   I've just read an amazing story. A teenage girl was the only survivor in a plane crash. It took place . . .

   ....

   ....

   ....

   ....

The present perfect

Rewrite the following sentences using the present perfect simple or present perfect continuous and the word in brackets. The first one has been done for you.

1. I didn't spend much time alone. (up to now)

Up to now, I haven't spent much time alone.

2. I invited Jacinta to my party. (just)

....

3. Did you see Paulo? (today)

....

4. Where are you staying? (this week)

....

5. She was travelling in Peru. (for the last two months)

....

Rewrite the following sentences in the present perfect passive. The first one has been done for you.

6. They reserved a ticket for you.

A ticket has been reserved for you.

7. They informed everyone about the meeting.

....

8. They elected Sabrina as head of the school council.

....

9. They recently promoted him to team captain.

....

Circle the correct verb form, A, B or C, to complete these sentences.

10. Have you ever .... to South America?

    A been going   **B** been   **C** went

11. Have you .... her for long?

    A been knowing   **B** knew   **C** known

12. I have always .... being alone.

    A liked   **B** been liking   **C** liking

Remember

- We often use the **present perfect simple** ('have/has' + past participle) with time expressions to talk about experiences we have had up to now. *Example:* I have seen this film before.

- The **present perfect continuous** ('have/has' + 'been' + present participle) is often used to talk about events that started in the past and continued up to now. *Example:* I have been learning English for two years.

Remember

We make the passive form of the present perfect simple with 'have/has' + 'been' + past participle. *Example:* The website has been updated.

A gift for Nik's brother

<u>Track 5.1</u> In the recording, you will hear Sian and Nik having a conversation in a shopping mall. As you listen, answer the questions.

For each question circle the correct answer A, B or C.

1. Why is Sian surprised to see Nik?

   A She thought Nik was away.

   B Nik doesn't like shopping.

   C She thought it was Nik's birthday.

2. What is Nik's brother interested in?

   A shopping

   B looking for clues

   C travelling to famous places

3. What does Nik's father think of the backpacking idea?

   A It is a joke.

   B He wants to go too.

   C It is all talk but no action.

Write answers to these questions.

4. What three things do we learn about Nik's brother from this conversation?

   ....

   ....

   ....

5. Help Nik choose a birthday present for her brother. Circle the gifts that Sian might have suggested based on the conversation.

A   B   C

The past perfect

Rewrite the sentences, using the words in brackets and the past perfect simple for the action that happened first. The first one has been done for you.

1. They looked in some shops. Sian arrived. (after)

   After Sian had arrived, they looked in some shops.

2. They began to feel hungry. They had some lunch. (because)

   ....

3. They went home. Nik bought a present. (as soon as)

   ....

4. Nik returned home. She hid the present under her bed. (after)

   ....

Circle the most suitable verb form, A or B, to complete the following sentences.

5. Nik .... for a present for about an hour when Sian arrived.

   A had looked   **B** had been looking

6. She .... anything yet.

   A hadn't found   **B** hadn't been finding

7. Sian .... that Nik's brother was going away.

   A hadn't told   **B** hadn't been told

Complete the second sentence using the past perfect simple or past perfect continuous. The first one has been done for you.

8. "I haven't seen you at the mall before."

   She said that she hadn't seen him at the mall before.

9. "I wasn't expecting to see Nik."

   Sian said ....

10. "I came to look for a present."

    Nik said ....

11. "My brother has been planning a big adventure."

    Nik explained ....

    ....

Alone in a different country

1. Nik's brother included Rio de Janiero, the Eiffel Tower and the Great Wall of China on his list of 'must-visit' places. What would be your top five places in the world to visit, if you could?

....

....

....

....

....

2. Choose one of the places from your list and imagine that you are going to travel there on your own. Research and make notes on the following:

- What country have you chosen, and what places are there to see?
- What arrangements would you need to make before you travel?
- What items would you take with you?
- What would you do to make sure you stay safe?

Write your notes here and then, if you can, share your plans with a friend or family member.

....

....

....

....

....

....

....

....

....

....

Home alone

Imagine that you are going to be at home alone one evening while the rest of the family go shopping. They suggest you invite a friend to spend the time with you, but you prefer to stay at home alone. What will you do while they are out? Will you:

- plan a pleasant surprise for your family?
- prepare a meal that you haven't cooked before?
- do something practical?
- get to work on something you have been putting off?
- or something else?

Write an email to a friend, explaining what you did and how you filled the time when you were alone.

....

....

....

....

....

....

....

....

....

....

....

....

Quiz

1. Which of the following injuries did Juliane receive when the plane crashed? Circle the correct answer A, B or C.

   A a sore head   **B** cuts, bruises and a broken collarbone   **c** a broken leg

2. In what two ways did the stream help Juliane survive?

   ....

   ....

3. Fill the gaps in the sentences with a present perfect simple or present perfect continuous form of the verb in brackets.

   a I .... always .... to go travelling. (want)

   b You look tired. .... you .... too hard? (work)

4. Name two places that Nik's brother wants to visit. (Listen to the Track 5.1 again if you need to.)

   ....

5. In **Track 5.1**, what two reasons does Sian give for not wanting to travel alone?

   ....

   ....

6. Change the following sentences into the passive, using the present perfect simple or past perfect simple.

   a He had sent the invitations a week before his birthday.

   ....

   b They have scheduled the meeting for next week.

   ....

7. Rewrite the following sentences as reported speech using 'she said' or 'he said' and the past perfect continuous.

   a "I haven't been feeling well."

   ....

   b "He has been planning the trip for quite a while."

   ....

8. What advice would you give to a friend about spending time alone?

   ....

⑥ Tomorrow's world

The world has changed a lot since your grandparents were the age you are now. Every day, there are new inventions. Link the invention on the left with what it could replace on the right.

mobile phone	portable cassette player
email	heat water on a stove
washing machine	using a video player
buy online	washing by hand
digital music	handwritten letter
streaming films	talking
using an electric kettle	go to a shop
text message	using an **encyclopaedia**
using the Internet	public telephone

Glossary

encyclopaedia books filled with information on many topics, arranged in alphabetical order

streaming downloading directly from the Internet

take for granted fail to properly notice or appreciate something

What do we have nowadays that we take for granted? Write one paragraph describing something that you have today that your grandparents didn't have. Do you agree we take this item for granted?

....

....

....

....

....

....

....

Tomorrow's World goes online

Read the article about *Tomorrow's World* and then answer the questions.

Tomorrow's World is a television show about science and technology which was first broadcast in the United Kingdom on 7 July 1965 and is now available online.

Many people used to watch it and were interested to see inventions for the future. Reporter Derek Cooper said at the time: "Can we expect a computer in every home?" Looking back, it is hard to believe that people could not imagine a time when computers would be used at home and phones were not connected to walls.

In 1965, James Burke was considered forward-thinking for discussing the possibility of **artificial** grass. Today, however, artificial grass is used in sporting locations and even in some people's gardens. These examples show us how quickly inventions change the world we live in.

Today, if we were going to make our own *Tomorrow's World* programme, what would we be discussing? Space colonisation, robots, different energy sources, cures for diseases and health issues, a **cyber** world full of new technology… the list has no end.

Technology is changing so fast that really anything is possible. This is an exciting time to live, with new things happening every day. Maybe we will have flying cars tomorrow – who knows?

For each of these questions circle the correct answer A, B or C.

1. What does the term 'forward-thinking' mean?

   A discussing the future　　　**B** finding out facts　　　**C** looking to the future

2. What is the programme *Tomorrow's World* about?

   A technology and engineering　　　**B** science and facts　　　**C** science and technology

Write answers to these questions.

3. What two things could people not imagine doing in the past according to the article?

   ....

   ....

4. Where might you find artificial grass, according to the article?

   ....

   ....

> ## Glossary
>
> **artificial** not natural, man-made
>
> **cyber** relating to computers and technology

Future forms

Circle the correct verb form, A, B or C, to complete the following sentences.

1. .... with you if you like.

   A I'll come   **B** I'm going to come   **C** I'm coming

2. He .... next week.

   A isn't working   **B** doesn't work   **C** won't have worked

3. The exam .... at 9 a.m. on Tuesday.

   A is   **B** will   **C** will have been

4. I .... a new mobile phone tomorrow.

   A am going to buy   **B** buy   **C** will be buying

5. By the time I am 19, I .... school.

   A will leave   **B** will be leaving   **C** will have left

6. Where do you think you .... in ten years' time?

   A are living   **B** will be living   **C** will have been living

Rewrite the following sentences in the passive.

7. Global warming will affect our lives.

   ....

8. We won't use paper money in 2050.

   ....

9. They are going to discuss wind power at the meeting.

   ....

   ....

Fill the gaps in the following sentences with the most suitable future form of the verb in brackets.

10. I don't think cars .... drivers in 2050. (need)

11. By 2030, I hope scientists .... cures for more diseases. (find)

12. In 2050, I expect people .... cars that can fly. (drive)

Remember

To talk about the future we can use:

- the **present simple** for future events that are part of a timetable

- the **present continuous** for future plans and arrangements

- **'will/shall' + verb** for things we believe to be true about the future, and to talk about offers, promises and decisions we make at the time of speaking

- **'be going to' + verb** to predict things and talk about future plans we have made

- the **future continuous** for things that will be happening at a particular time in the future

- the **future perfect** for actions that will have happened or be complete by a certain time in the future.

Radio special: The first 'thinking' robots

Track 6.1 You are going to listen to a radio interview with the first thinking robots Henry and Henrietta. As you are listening, make notes about how Henry and Henrietta help people. Then listen again and answer the questions.

For each of these questions, circle the correct answer A, B or C.

1. What does the word 'assist' mean?

   A help   **B** manage   **C** control

2. Henry says "I can even travel for you" to show that he can:

   A only travel

   B assist you very little

   C travel and do lots of things for you

3. When Henrietta says "all in one" she means she can:

   A care for you

   B be a friend to you

   C play the part of many people to you

4. How does Henrietta's employer attend meetings all over the world?

   A by travelling   **B** by computer   **C** by phone

5. What is included in the robots' two-year contracts?

   A health checks and information backups

   B battery and health tests

   C thinking tests

6. Henry and Henrietta are different from other robots because they have been designed to:

   A have emotions   **B** feel pain   **C** connect with humans

Glossary

backups computer files that are saved so no information is lost

connect with form an understanding

errands journeys to take a message or do something

virtually in a way that uses a computer to do or see something

Write an answer to this question.

7. Write a short paragraph, describing the future plans for robots.

....

....

....

....

Phrasal and prepositional verbs

1. Match the phrasal verbs on the left with their meanings on the right. One has been done for you.

miss out	tell someone about some information
set out	to eat in a restaurant
turn out	be easy to see
point out	not include someone or something
leave out	end in a successful way
eat out	happen in a particular way
stand out	not do something that you would enjoy
work out	start a journey

2. Fill the gaps in the email below with words from the box. You may need to use some of the words more than once.

> up   away   in   off   out   on   with

Hi Henry

My employer's meeting has been called ...., so I don't need to go .... tomorrow. But I still need to call .... to her office to pick .... some papers. I hope the security guard will let me .... this time. How are you getting on .... your family? My family certainly believes .... keeping me busy! I've spent a lot of time this week tidying .... the children's toys and putting .... their clothes. I have worked .... how to back .... my computer's memory now – thanks for passing .... that information.

Henrietta

3. Write four sentences using each of the following verbs.

> set off   set up   put off   put up

....

....

....

....

A new invention for tomorrow's world

You are going to plan a short interview with an inventor about his or her latest invention. You will play the role of the inventor, answering the questions below. Research online for ideas and use your imagination to think of what the invention is.

Answer the following questions:

• What has been invented?

....

....

....

• What facts can you find about the new invention?

....

....

....

• How will it work?

....

....

....

• What can it be used for?

....

....

....

• Who will use it?

....

....

....

Now practise answering the interview questions aloud. Try to answer the interview questions without using your notes. If you cannot remember what to say, think of ways to fill in the gaps. If possible, role play the interview with a friend or family member (they could read the questions for you to answer).

Writing a short story

You are going to fill the gaps in a fictional short story called 'Tomorrow's World'. Choose from the words below and write the correct number in each box.

☐ first   ☐ with

☐ hear   ☐ temperature

☐ visiting   ☐ begin

☐ appeared   ☐ sound

☐ colony   ☐ warmed

Mia woke to the ...(1)... of her room quietly saying "Wake up Mia, it's time to ...(2)... your day". The sun's rays gently ...(3)... her face and the ...(4)... was slowly raised to help Mia feel comfortable. She could ...(5)... the sound of the water as the shower turned on, ready for the ...(6)... shower of the day. Quickly, Mia opened the small window and looked out on the rest of the space ...(7).... The image of her mother ...(8)... on the screen in front of her, it was as if she was in the room ...(9)... Mia. "Are you going to fly with us? Remember we're ...(10)... Earth today."

Now, continue the story by writing the next paragraph.

Mia could not believe she had forgotten that today was the day she would see Earth again . . .

....

....

....

....

....

....

....

....

....

....

Quiz

For each question, circle the correct answer A, B or C.

1. What does the word 'invention' mean?

    A something which has been created or made

    B something which has been talked about

    C something which has been written

2. According to the article on *Tomorrow's World*, which of the following had not been invented in 1965?

    A television   **B** computers   **C** mobile phones

3. When was *Tomorrow's World* first broadcast?

    A July 7 1965   **B** July 6 1975   **C** July 5 1986

4. According to the article, in what way is *Tomorrow's World* most interesting to us today?

    A We can see which inventions for the future came true and which didn't.

    B We can see how people designed things.

    C We can see how people have changed.

5. Circle the sentence with the correct future form, A, B or C.

    A By 2050, scientists will found new sources of energy.

    B This time next week, we will be finished our exams.

    C Maybe in future there will be robots that can think.

6. According to Track 6.1, why have thinking robots been created?

    A to allow humans to work more

    B to allow humans to deal with other things

    C to allow humans to do nothing

7. Use the following verbs in three sentences of your own.

    sort out   pick up   rely on

    ....

    ....

    ....

8. Is it important for humans to keep in control of technology? Give reasons for your answer.

    ....

    ....

    ....

What lies beneath our feet

Have you ever travelled or explored underground

- in a subway
- in a tunnel
- some other way?

If you have never been underground, try to imagine what it would be like.

1. Make a list of words and phrases that describe how you felt, what you heard, and what you saw.

....

....

....

....

....

2. Write a short paragraph about a journey that includes going through a tunnel, describing the moment that you go from open air to darkness. See how many of the words and phrases from your list you can include.

....

....

....

....

....

....

....

....

....

....

Volcanoes

Read this short text about volcanoes and then answer the questions that follow.

A volcano is usually a hole in the top of a mountain. It provides a way for molten lava beneath the Earth's crust to force its way up to the surface. When this happens the volcano is said to be **erupting**. Extremely hot rocks are thrown into the air and rivers of molten lava run down the side of the volcano, burning everything in their path.

There are three main categories of volcano: active – these are the ones that regularly erupt; dormant ('sleeping') – these haven't erupted recently but may do so at any time; and extinct ('have died out') – these were active in the past but are no longer expected to erupt.

Volcanic eruptions are nature's way of solving the build-up of **pressure** beneath the Earth's crust. At the same time they are a great danger, and in the past have destroyed whole communities. A famous example is the Roman city of Pompeii which was buried by an eruption almost 2,000 years ago.

Volcanoes are one of the wonders of nature: spectacular sights that need to be treated with respect and care.

For each question circle the correct answer A, B or C.

1. What happens when a volcano erupts?

   A Rivers are thrown in the air.

   B The Earth's crust comes to the surface.

   C Molten lava comes to the surface.

2. What is the term for a volcano that is no longer expected to erupt?

   A active　　　　　**B** dormant　　　　　**C** extinct

3. Why do we have to treat volcanoes with care?

   A They are spectacular sights.　　　**B** They have great destructive power.

   C They are easily destroyed.

Write answers to these questions.

4. List four adjectives that might be used to describe a volcano erupting.

   ....　　...

   ....　　...

5. Use the information to write a short description of a volcano erupting. See how many of your listed adjectives you can include.

   ....

Glossary

erupting suddenly throwing out smoke, fire and melted rocks

pressure force produced by a liquid or gas when it pushes against an area

Questions

Rewrite the following statements as 'yes/no' questions. The first one has been done for you.

1. This volcano has become dormant.

Has this volcano become dormant?

2. The eruption buried the whole town.

....

3. Volcanoes can be found under the sea.

....

4. This volcano will erupt soon.

....

Turn the following statements into questions by adding a question tag. The first one has been done for you.

5. This volcano erupted recently.

The volcano erupted recently, didn't it?

6. The volcano won't erupt again.

....

7. You could visit Pompeii next year.

....

8. Serena has seen a volcano.

....

Write 'wh–' questions for these answers using the question words in brackets.

9. He is going to Italy to visit Pompeii. (why)

....

10. The volcano that buried Pompeii was Mount Vesuvius. (which)

....

Remember

To make a 'yes/no' question, we usually use the word order: auxiliary/modal verb + subject + main verb. In the present simple or past simple we use the auxiliary 'do/does/did'.

Remember

- We make question tags using an auxiliary/modal verb + pronoun. If the verb in the question is 'be' we use 'be' in the question tag.
- We use a negative verb in the question tag if the verb in the statement is positive, and a positive verb in the tag when the verb in the statement is negative.

Remember

- To ask for more information, we ask 'wh–' questions beginning with question words such as 'why', 'what' or 'when'.
- When a question word is the subject or part of the subject of a question, we do not use 'do/does/did'. *Example:* Which volcano erupted? (not 'Which volcano did erupt?')

An invitation to go caving

 **Track 7.1** In the recording you will hear part of a telephone conversation between two students. Zoe has phoned her friend Kristin to invite her to join the college caving club on a weekend away. Listen to the conversation and answer the questions.

Glossary

caving exploring caves

over-trousers waterproof trousers worn over other trousers to keep them dry

trial a test, often free, before someone decides to buy something

For each question, circle the correct answer A, B or C.

1. Why would the caving weekend be free for Kristin?

   A It is free for anyone who wants to go.

   B It is free for anyone new to caving.

   C It is free because Kristin already has all the clothes and equipment.

2. How far underground does the caving group usually go?

   A no more than 100 metres

   B more than 100 metres

   C it depends on how long the rope is

3. What does Zoe offer to lend Kristin if she'll come?

| A | B | C |

Write an answer to this question.

4. Listen to **Track 7.1** again, then explain in your own words what caving is like.

....

....

....

....

Reported speech, indirect and embedded questions

Complete the sentences in reported speech. The first one has been done for you.

1. "I am a bit scared."

   Kristin confessed to *being a bit scared*.

2. "I will make the arrangements."

   Zoe promised ....

3. "Someone has dropped out."

   She explained ....

4. "I am sorry, but I'm nervous."

   Kristin apologised for ....

Answer this question.

5. Fill the gaps in the following email with the correct form of a reporting verb from the box.

admit to	assure	mention
agree	offer	encourage

   Hi Kai
   I .... to Kristin that there is a spare place on the caving trip. She .... knowing nothing about caving. I .... her that caving is safe and .... to lend her a helmet. I .... her to come and she has .... to think about it.
   Zoe

Complete the following indirect and embedded questions.

6. "How deep is the cave?"

   Could you tell me .... ?

7. "Has she been caving?"

   I wondered ....

Remember

After reporting verbs, we often use:

- **the 'to' infinitive.**
  Examples: tell, offer, promise, encourage
- **a 'that' clause.**
  Examples: mention, explain, remind, assure
- **a gerund (–ing form).**
  Examples: confess to, admit (to), apologise for

Remember

In **reported, indirect** and **embedded questions**, we put the subject before the verb and we do not use 'do/does/did'. We do not change the tense in indirect and embedded questions.

Examples: "Does she want to go?" ⟶ He asked if she wanted to go. Do you know if she wants to go? ⟶ I wonder if she wants to go.

Exploring an area you know

1. Think about the area where you live, or another area that you know well. What places would be interesting to explore? How many of the following can be found? Tick all that apply.

In your nearest town or city:

☐ historic buildings

☐ museums

☐ parkland

☐ subways

In the countryside nearby:

☐ mountains

☐ caves

☐ coastline

☐ rivers

2. Now make your own list of interesting places to explore.

....

....

....

3. Prepare a talk to give to your class about the opportunities for exploring near you, or in an area you know well. Remember to include some underground attractions if you can.

Write some notes to help you with your talk.

....

....

....

....

....

....

....

....

....

....

....

When you have finished, practise your talk aloud with a friend or family member.

Surprise find at local site

A team of volunteers has discovered a secret store of coins, furniture and cooking pots that experts think are at least a thousand years old.

Read the text below, and for each number, circle the correct word from the list.

> The items were found by accident ...(1)... one of the students working on a ...(2)... site decided to try a patch of ground not previously dug over. As she ...(3)... she hit something hard, which she ...(4)... was a large pot full of gold ...(5).... She called her friends over and ...(6)... they had unearthed several other pots and the ...(7)... of some old stools and even ...(8)... of a chair. The scientist leading the ...(9)... arrived and confirmed that they had ...(10)... a very special discovery.

1.	before	when	instead	besides
2.	nearly	nasty	nearby	next
3.	dug	dig	is digging	has dug
4.	discovered	uncovered	recovered	covered
5.	pencils	money	tins	coins
6.	suddenly	soon	often	instead
7.	remains	rest	left	pans
8.	top	bit	rest	parts
9.	way	team	race	dance
10.	lost	found	made	taken

Quiz

1. What does it mean if a volcano is 'dormant'?

....

....

2. Give a famous example of a dangerous volcano, according to the article on page 51.

....

3. Turn the following statements into questions by adding question tags.

a She visited Pompeii last year.

....

b This volcano is active.

....

4. Name two safety procedures that Zoe mentions to Kristin in Track 7.1.

....

....

5. Give two reasons why Zoe thinks Kristin might enjoy the caving weekend.

....

....

6. What does Zoe say can be seen inside the caves they explore?

....

7. Rewrite the following questions, correcting the mistakes.

a Where lava does come from?

....

b Where the largest active volcano in the world is?

....

8. Rewrite the following questions as embedded or indirect questions.

a "Has she been caving?"

I wonder ....

b "Where is the cave?"

I don't know ....

Food and culture

The Burns Supper is a **traditional** festival in Scotland that celebrates the life of the famous poet Robert Burns (1759–1796). Although 'supper' is usually a small informal meal, the Burns Supper is often a formal dinner which includes eating traditional Scottish foods such as **haggis**, reading the poetry of Robert Burns and Scottish dancing to the sound of the **bagpipes**.

You are organising a meal for your friends and family to celebrate a traditional day in your country. Create invitations for your guests using the checklist below to help you.

- ☐ Name and address of sender
- ☐ Name and address of guest
- ☐ When?
- ☐ Who?
- ☐ Date your guest should respond by
- ☐ Today's date
- ☐ What?
- ☐ Where?
- ☐ Why?
- ☐ Your name at the end

Glossary

bagpipes a wind instrument, played by a musician called a piper

haggis a pudding containing the heart, liver and lungs of a sheep

traditional relating to something which has been done for a long time

(Date:) .... (Guest's address:) ....

....

....

(Your address:) ....

....

Dear ....

You are invited to ....

....

....

Please respond by: ....

....

A lesson in manners

Read the following school magazine article and then answer the questions.

This week we will be looking at how to act when you are invited to a meal, especially when you are visiting another country where the culture is different. It is important to know the correct **manners** so that your behaviour does not seem rude towards your **host**, your family or other guests.

If you have been invited to a meal, always try to arrive on time. In most cultures, it is **unacceptable** to be too early or late for a meal.

When the meal is served, you should usually wait for the host to begin eating before you start. Keep your elbows off the table. Do not take pictures of your food and Tweet them. In fact, it is not polite to accept calls or text messages unless there is an emergency.

You may find there are dishes which you have never seen before and you should eat at least a little bite of everything. This is a great opportunity to try new foods. Ask politely about the food and how it has been made. Feel free to say how tasty the food is because everybody likes to know their food has been enjoyed.

You should not leave straight after you have eaten. You should stay and talk with your host and other guests. Finally, make sure to thank the host at the end of the meal.

These are just some of the things that you'll need to think about, and it's always good to learn about the customs of a country before you visit. But if in doubt, copy what others around you are doing!

Glossary

host (male or female) the person who sent the invitation

manners the polite way of behaving with other people

unacceptable too bad to be accepted or allowed

Write answers to the following questions.

1. Why is it important to know how to act during a meal in another country? ....

    ....

2. What should you do when the meal is served? ....

    ....

3. What should you do after you finish your meal?

    ....

Gerunds and noun phrases

Fill the gaps in the following sentences using gerunds made from a verb in the box.

leave	eat	keep
arrive	answer	invite

1. Thank you for .... us.

2. Avoid .... your phone during the meal.

3. .... very late might be considered rude.

4. .... a little bit of everything is polite.

5. Remember to thank your host before ....

6. I need to practise .... my elbows off the table.

Answer this question.

7. In questions 1–6, which sentences include a gerund that is:

   a the subject of the verb?

   ....

   b the object of the verb?

   ....

   c the object of a preposition?

   ....

Put the following words in the right order to make noun phrases.

8. went to/we/on Saturday/that formal meal

   ....

9. last week/all the guests/the event/who attended

   ....

10. the invitations/a few of/we sent/yesterday/that

    ....

11. the text message/while I was eating/to me/you sent

    ....

Remember

- Gerunds (–ing forms used as nouns) can be the subject or object of a verb.
- Like verbs, gerunds can sometimes have an object. The whole gerund phrase (gerund + object) can be the subject or object of a verb. *Examples:* (subject) Cooking is fun. (object) She enjoys cooking.

Remember

We often use gerunds as the object of a preposition. *Example:* I am looking forward to seeing you.

Remember

A noun phrase can include words before and after a noun. We use the following word order: quantifier/determiner (+ adjective) + noun + other words such as a prepositional phrase or relative clause.

Janssons Frestelse

<u>Track 8.1</u> You are going to listen to a chef describing a recipe for 'Janssons Frestelse' (Jansson's Temptation), a Swedish dish which usually includes a selection of fish, cheese, vegetables and meat. As you are listening, make notes and listen for the main points, as well as specific details, and then fill the gaps in the recipe below.

Preparation and cooking time: around one hour

.... 6 people

Ingredients

9–10 .... sized potatoes

30 g butter, ...

1 onion .... sliced

150 ml cream

150 ml milk

14 **anchovies** or **smoked** salmon if you .... less salty fish

1 tablespoon dried breadcrumbs

Method

1. .... the oven to 220 degrees Celsius.

2. Peel the potatoes and .... into thin sticks.

3. .... the onion in a saucepan with oil or butter until soft.

4. Spread the onions on the bottom of the dish. Place the anchovies on top of the onions and add the potatoes on top of the anchovies.

5. Mix the cream with the milk and pour in.

6. .... the breadcrumbs together with the .... butter and **sprinkle** over the top of the potatoes.

7. .... onto a baking tray and bake until the dish has turned a golden brown.

Glossary

anchovies small salty fish

smoked when fish is cooked using smoke

sprinkle add a light amount

temptation something you really want to eat

Now answer the following questions.

1. Which two vegetables are used to make this dish?

   A carrots and potatoes   **B** potatoes and onions   **C** milk and onions

2. Where can anchovies usually be found?

   A in the sea   **B** underground   **C** nesting in trees

Infinitives and gerunds

1. Complete the conversation, adding 'to' where it is needed. Leave the gap blank if 'to' isn't necessary.

Jemma: Would you .... like .... invite some friends for dinner? I'm keen .... make the dish the chef told us about.

Sandro: Yes, I'd .... love that. I can .... help you with the cooking if you .... like.

Jemma: It's kind of you .... offer, but I .... think I'll be able .... manage. The dish sounds easy .... prepare.

Sandro: Do you .... have all the ingredients?

Jemma: We .... need .... buy some potatoes. Would it be possible for you .... get some?

Sandro: No problem. I'd be happy .... buy some.

Rewrite the following sentences using 'it' + a form of 'be' + the adjective in brackets. The first one has been done for you.

2. I can't come to dinner this evening. (not possible)

It's not possible for me to come to dinner this evening.

3. You should heat the oven first. (important)

....

4. I can't decide whether to go. (difficult)

....

Underline the correct verb form in the following sentences.

5. He was hoping *(to be invited/to invite)* to the meal.

6. I can't wait *(to hear/to be heard)* how the dinner went.

7. She was expecting *(to receive/to be received)* a letter today.

Fill in the gaps in the following sentences with the correct form of the verb in brackets.

8. Try not .... the onions. (burn)

9. She is keen on .... for her friends. (cook)

10. I remember .... this dish before. (try)

11. Remember .... the oven first. (heat)

Remember

We use the 'to' infinitive:

- after many adjectives. *Example:* I was **glad to see** you.

- after 'it' + a form of 'be' + adjective. *Examples:* **It is important (for you) to arrive** on time. **It was sensible (of you) to accept** the invitation.

- after many verbs. *Example:* He **promised to come** with me.

Remember

To make a passive 'to' infinitive, we use 'to be' + past participle. *Examples:* to be chosen, to be told

Remember

- Some verbs are followed by a gerund rather than the 'to' infinitive.

- Some verbs can be followed by a 'to' infinitive or a gerund. Sometimes there is a difference in meaning.

- After a preposition, we always use a gerund rather than the 'to' infinitive.

More lessons in manners

In Germany, you should always arrive on time and bring a small gift.

In India, it is important never to eat with your left hand!

Traditionally, in Italy, there is the appetiser, the first course, main course, a side dish and the dessert.

In Thailand, it is traditional for the oldest ladies of the group to order the food.

1. List three dining customs that are important in your country, using one or more words from the vocabulary below in each example you give.

traditions	invitation	habits	society	background
napkin	course	host	guests	knives and forks

a ....

b ....

c ....

2. Your English friend Rosie is visiting your country, and she is going for dinner with some new friends. Complete the conversation below on how to behave when dining in your country.

Rosie: Hello, can you help me? I am going for dinner with some new friends tonight. How should I behave?

You: Of course, first of all, you should ....

Rosie: What time should I arrive?

You: ....

Rosie: Do I need to take a gift?

You: ....

Rosie: Is there anything else I need to know?

You: ....

Rosie: Thank you, I am ready now to meet my friends!

Role play the conversation with a friend of family member if you can.

Celebrations and food

Read the following example of a menu that might be served at a traditional Burns Supper.

Burns Night Supper Menu

25 January

To celebrate Burns Night

Starter:

'Barley broth' (fish soup)

Main course:

Highland beef stew

Haggis with neeps and tatties (root vegetables and potatoes)

Dessert:

Fruit loaf

Traditional shortbread biscuits

Tea and coffee

Research different celebrations around the world, then choose one and write a paragraph to describe the celebration and the food that will be eaten. You could also design a menu for your chosen celebration.

Think about the following:

- What is the celebration?
- Where is it held?
- Why is it celebrated?
- How is it celebrated?
- What food is eaten?

....

....

....

....

....

Writing ....

64

Quiz

1. Which activities would you expect to be doing at a Burns Night Supper? Circle the correct answer A, B or C.

  A watching films and reading poetry

  B reading poetry and dancing

  C drawing and writing

2. The Burns Supper is a traditional festival in which country? Circle the correct answer A, B or C.

  A England   **B** Scotland   **C** Ireland

3. Fill the gaps in the following sentences with the correct form of the verb in brackets.

  a I checked my diary before .... the invitation. (accept)

  b If you can't help .... late, you should let your host know. (be)

  c .... food with friends is fun. (share)

4. What does 'temptation' mean in 'Jansson's Temptation'? Circle the correct answer A, B or C.

  A you really want to eat it   **B** main dish   **C** perfect meal

5. According to the article on page 59, what should you do when you are served new food in another country? Give two examples.

....

....

6. Circle the correct words from a–d to fill the gaps in the sentence below.

When you are ...**(a)**... to a meal, it is important to know the correct ...**(b)**... or your ...**(c)**... might find your behaviour ...**(d)**... .

  a invented   attended   invited   intended

  b manners   mention   method   ingredients

  c guest   host   chef   customs

  d acceptable   unacceptable

7. Underline the noun phrases in the following sentences.

  a I must reply to that party invitation that I received this morning.

  b Did you receive my email about the dinner that Reena is hosting next week?

8. Underline the correct verb form in the following sentences.

  a She would prefer (*to be given/to give*) the results by her teacher.

  b Don't forget (*to lay/laying*) the table.

  c She thanked him for (*to help/helping*) her.

People who changed the world

1. What do we mean when we say someone 'changed the world'? Tick the boxes that you think apply.

   ☐ They invented something that made a difference to people.

   ☐ They were celebrities.   ☐ They changed people's lives.

   ☐ They made a lot of money. ☐ They were a good example.

   Now add some suggestions of your own:

   ....

   ....

2. Who would be your choice of a 'world changer', past or present? Explain briefly why you think they might be called this. Remember to include some of the characteristics you ticked in question 1.

   ....

   ....

   ....

   ....

3. Now imagine what the world would be like without this person. Write down some ideas, using the following questions to help you.

   • Would people's lives be better or worse?

   • Would people still be able to travel or communicate in the same way?

   • What else might not have happened or been invented?

   • How might your life be different today?

   ....

   ....

   ....

   ....

   ....

   ....

Johannes Gutenberg

Read this article about the invention of printing and then answer the questions.

One invention that changed the world dramatically and forever was the printing **press**. The man responsible for this great advance was a German **blacksmith** called Johannes Gutenberg, who lived in Germany over 500 years ago and began to experiment with printing in 1438.

Using his skills as a blacksmith, Gutenberg built a piece of **machinery** that enabled the copying of pages to make a printed book. Before this, most books had been slowly and carefully copied by hand, a process that was full of error as well as very slow. Printing had actually started years earlier in China, where copies were printed out using carved wood blocks, but these took a long time and only a single copy could be produced at one time.

Gutenberg changed all that by replacing the wooden lettering with metal **type**. Again, this had been used a little in China many years earlier. But Gutenberg experimented with different metals and **forged** separate letters that were easily moved around. . . .

The printing of books had begun.

For each question circle the correct answer A, B or C.

1. Before the invention of printing, books were _____
   A carved in wood   B written out by hand   C not made

2. What job did Gutenberg have?
   A farmer   B wood carver   C blacksmith

3. Where did printing first begin?
   A China   B Germany   C France

Write answers to these questions.

4. What important change did Gutenberg make to the letters?

   ....

   ....

5. What was the importance of Gutenberg's invention? Write a short paragraph under the heading: 'How Johannes Gutenberg changed the world'.

   ....

   ....

   ....

   ....

Glossary

blacksmith a person who makes things from metal

forged made by heating metal and shaping it with a hammer

machinery one or more machines

press a piece of equipment that pushes down hard on an object

type letters used in printing

Conjunctions and modal verbs

Fill the gaps in the following sentences with the correct conjunction from the brackets.

1. He used movable type .... printing would be quicker. (though/so that)

2. Books were sometimes copied by hand, ... it took a long time. (whereas/even though)

3. At first, he didn't know .... metal was better than wood. (whether/either)

4. Gutenberg was .... a printer but also a blacksmith. (both/not only)

5. .... books could be printed quickly, they became cheaper. (Because/So)

6. .... Gutenberg invented the printing press, books were very expensive. (Before/Because)

For each number in the conversation, choose the correct verb form from the list below.

Jima: I have just tried to ring Rana but she didn't answer. She ...(7)... left her phone at home.

Sunita: She rang me five minutes ago, so she ...(8)... forgotten it.

Jima: She ...(9)... turned it off since then. She's probably busy.

Sunita: You ...(10)... left a message.

Jima: Yes, I ...(11)... thought of that.

7.	should have	must have	can have
8.	mustn't have	shouldn't have	can't have
9.	might have	should have	can have
10.	may have	could have	can have
11.	should have	must have	may have

Remember

We use conjunctions to talk about:

- additional information (and, both ... and, not only ... and)
- contrasting ideas (although, whereas, even though)
- reasons and results (because, since, as, so)
- choices and alternatives (or, whether ... or (not), either ... or)
- time (before, after, until, as soon as)
- purpose (so, so that, so as, in order that).

Remember

We often use a modal verb + 'have' + past participle to:

- say how sure we are that something happened. *Examples:* (certain) They must have told him. (not certain) They might/may/could have told him.
- say we are sure something didn't happen. *Example:* She can't/couldn't have told him.
- criticise someone's actions or express regret. *Example:* You could/might/should/shouldn't have told him.

The first to reach the top

Track 9.1 In the recording you will hear a news bulletin reporting the successful climbing of Mount Everest. Listen to the announcement and then answer the questions.

For each question, circle the correct answer A, B or C.

1. Where is the mountain climbers' base camp?

   A at the foot of the Himalayan mountains

   B at the top of the Himalayan mountains

   C high in the Himalayan mountains

2. How many men reached the top of Mount Everest that day?

   A one   **B** two   **C** three

3. What did they do when they reached the top of Everest?

A	**B**	**C**

> # Glossary
>
> **base camp** where the main team is staying
>
> **Sherpa** a member of a Himalayan people known for their mountain climbing skills
>
> **summit** the top of a mountain

Write answers to these questions.

4. If you could meet Hillary and Norgay, what two questions would you ask them about their achievement?

   ....

   ....

5. Listen again to the news bulletin, making notes. Then write a short paragraph reporting the achievement for a newspaper, giving the main facts.

   ....

   ....

   ....

   ....

   ....

Conditional sentences

1. Match the two clauses in the following sentences. One has been done for you.

If you reach the top   unless you wear a hat.

Water becomes ice   if you don't go alone.

You will be cold   if it freezes.

You will be safer   you will see a long way.

If you like sport   don't go climbing.

If the weather is bad   you might enjoy climbing.

Circle the correct verb form, A, B or C, to complete the following sentences.

2. If you .... a mountain climber, what would you say?

   A had met   **B** met   **C** are meeting

3. If we had lots of money, we .... go to Nepal.

   A will   **B** could   **C** can

4. If I .... you, I would wear warm clothes.

   A will be   **B** were   **C** am

5. If I reached base camp, I would .... very proud.

   A be   **B** to be   **C** will be

Rewrite the following sentences using the third conditional. The first one has been done for you.

6. If I reached the top, I would take lots of photos.

If I had reached the top, I would have taken lots of photos.

7. If you climbed a bit higher, you would reach the top.

....

....

....

8. If only it was not so cold, we could go climbing.

....

....

....

Planning and giving a talk

You are going to give a short talk to your class about a world changer who you admire. This can be someone you have read about already or another person of your choice.

Research the person you have chosen so that you will have enough facts to make your talk interesting. Remember to include an introduction and a conclusion.

Put together your talk, explaining:

- who you have chosen, and where they are from
- how this person changed the world
- what qualities you admire in this person.

Make some notes below to help you with your talk. If you can, practise your talk at home or with a friend or family member.

....

....

....

....

....

....

....

....

....

....

....

....

....

....

'Today I met . . .'

Write a blog about the day you met one of the world changers you have read about. This can either be someone famous from the past or someone alive today. Choose a person you have not written about already and use your imagination to describe this meeting.

Think about the following questions.

- Who is the person that you met, and how did they change the world?
- How and where did the meeting take place? If the person is from the past, perhaps one of you has travelled in time?
- What happened? What did you talk about? Did they give you any advice?
- How did you feel about meeting them?

Write your blog in the space below. Write 100–120 words.

Today I met ....

....

....

....

....

....

....

....

....

....

....

....

....

When you have written your piece, check your spelling and punctuation. If possible, ask a friend or family member to read it.

Quiz

1. According to the article on page 67, how long ago did Johannes Gutenberg live? Circle the correct answer A, B or C.

   A exactly 500 years ago   **B** less than 500 years ago   **C** more than 500 years ago

2. What two problems with copying books by hand are described in the article?

   ....

   ....

3. Fill the gaps in the following sentences with a suitable conjunction.

   a Gutenberg tried out different metals .... he wanted to find out which was best.

   b You can .... print the book or copy it by hand.

4. Who were the first successful climbers of Mount Everest? (Listen to Track 9.1 again if you need to.)

   ....

5. Give two reasons why Colonel Hunt was pleased to see the climbers back at camp.

   ....

   ....

6. Which flags did the climbers place on the top of Everest?

   ....

   ....

7. Fill the gaps in the following sentences with the correct verb form from the brackets.

   a When it is cold, I .... my gloves. (wore/wear)

   b If you .... to the news, you would have heard the announcement. (listen/had listened)

8. Write a short paragraph explaining how you might become someone who changes the world.

   ....

   ....

   ....

   ....

Read the following weather reports and, for each one, write a headline for a newspaper.

1. A bitterly cold Arctic wind will bring freezing temperatures for up to two weeks. This will follow a period of unusually warm temperatures and sunshine, which is expected to last until the end of the week. Experts have warned that this period will not last, however, and temperatures will drop to below freezing by early next week. There may even be snow in some parts of the country.

....

....

2. We expect frost and snow in the north of the country, and the freezing temperatures are predicted to last until the end of the year. Bands of rain or snow, occasionally heavy, will move south-east next week, bringing much colder conditions to all parts of the country.

....

....

3. The weather is getting warmer! Temperatures over the next week are forecast to climb to an amazing 45° C. People are advised to stay indoors and drink plenty of water. Such high temperatures are not expected at this time of the year; summer has arrived very suddenly.

....

....

4. Thunderstorms and heavy rain are expected to reach all parts of the country by this evening. These should help to lower the temperature as well as humidity levels. Temperatures are expected to remain high all week but southerly winds will provide a cooling effect.

....

....

Summary writing

Read the following article about what causes thunder and lightning and then answer the questions that follow.

---

www.weatherinfo.co.uk

What causes a thunder and lightning storm?

Dramatic weather happens all over the world. Among the most common examples of sudden weather are thunder and lightning storms, recognised by loud booming noises known as 'thunder' and flashes of light known as 'lightning'. It is estimated that lightning strikes happen somewhere on Earth every 44 seconds. The Island of Java has 220 thunder storms a year and is thought to be the most thundery place on Earth.

Thunderstorms are created when warm air meets cold air. As the warm air rises it becomes cooler and this causes water droplets to form, creating clouds. As the warm air rises, the water droplets become bigger and colder and form ice crystals. When these become too heavy for the air, they fall as hail or frozen rain. The lighter and heavier crystals mix together and form a positive and negative energy. When the positive and negative energy meet, a flash of lightening is formed. The boom of the thunder is caused by air which has been heated up very quickly. Thunderstorms often happen in places where it is hot and humid, and over land rather than oceans.

---

1. What are thunderstorms?

....

2. What causes thunderstorms to form?

....

....

....

3. Where do thunderstorms form?

....

Now, using your notes, write a summary about thunderstorms in your notebook. Write 70–80 words and use your own words as far as possible.

Weather news

Read the article about new technology in weather forecasting.

New technology allows winter weather to be predicted more accurately.

"Nice day today"; "It's getting colder, isn't it?"; "A bit breezy now!" People in the United Kingdom are always talking about the weather, because it is very unpredictable: it seems sometimes that four seasons can happen in the space of 10 minutes.

But a new £97 million pound supercomputer may soon put a stop to these conversations, during the winter season at least. Scientists believe that this supercomputer will accurately forecast weather in the Atlantic, which is largely responsible for British winter weather, up to one year in advance.

Dr Nick Dunstone, from the Met Office, says the supercomputer "will be very useful for people who have to deal with risk. This is an exciting first step in developing useful winter climate predictions on longer timescales."

Unfortunately, it is not currently possible to predict weather all year round, as the weather is controlled by more complex factors throughout the rest of the year. But if you're wondering what the weather will be like next winter, you may not have so long to wait!

Source: adapted from *The Met Office can now predict winter weather one year in advance*, www.telegraph.co.uk

Answer these questions.

1. Match the words below with the correct definition.

unpredictable	correctly
accurately	one thing, of a few, that has an effect on a situation
complex	changing so often that you never know what will happen next
factor	with lots of different, connected parts

2. Choose a phrase in the article that describes the weather in the United Kingdom.

....

3. According to the article, what will help to predict the winter weather going forward?

....

4. According to the article, why can't summer weather be predicted?

....

....

Weather around the world today

 Track 10.1. Listen to a radio programme called "Weather around the world today", then for each question below, fill in the missing information in the numbered space.

Auckland, New Zealand

Temperature: **(1)**..........................°C-20°C

Weather:

• cloudy

• a light shower of **(2)**..........................
  in the afternoon

• **(3)**.......................... rising

Cape Town, South Africa

Temperature: **(4)**..........................°C

Weather:

• increasing **(5)**.......................... all week

• clear blue skies

• no **(6)**..........................

• pleasant cooling **(7)**..........................

Mexico City, Mexico

Temperature: **(8)**..........................

Weather:

• sunny

• light **(9)**.......................... expected
  this afternoon

• more comfortable temperatures

Moscow, Russia

Temperature: 1°C

• winter is coming

• more cloud through the week

• a chance of **(10)**..........................
  tomorrow

• cold south-west winds

• sun by the weekend

Now listen to the recording again and write answers to the questions below.

1. What is the good news for Auckland, New Zealand?

....

2. What two things does the presenter wish the listeners?

....

....

3. What new device does the presenter tell the listeners about?

....

Weather at home

You are going to prepare a presentation about where you live, to persuade someone else to visit.

Answer these questions. You may need to use the Internet or a library, or to ask someone you know, to find the answers.

- Describe the place – try to be persuasive.

  ....

  ....

  ....

- What is there to see in your country?

  ....

- What is the weather like?

  ....

- When is the best time to visit, and why?

  ....

  ....

- What is the highest average temperature?

  ....

- What is the lowest average temperature?

  ....

- What is the average rainfall?

  ....

- What is the average humidity level?

  ....

- Is the country affected by severe weather (e.g. flooding, heat, storms)?

  ....

  ....

Descriptive writing

In his painting "Place Vendôme in the Rain", the painter Edouard Léon Cortès shows the weather in Paris, France on a winter's day. Fill in the gaps in the description below with the correct word from the boxes.

> moments   business   reflections   create

Edouard Cortès painted this picture of Place Vendôme in the Rain, in Paris, France. Cortès used the rain and the .... in the puddles to bring to life every day .... of people doing .... their on a rainy day in Paris. The painting uses dark colours to .... the feeling of a rainy day.

Now look at Vincent Van Gogh's painting "Sower with Setting Sun" and write your own description. Try to include one example of each: sensory description, powerful adjective and verb, and simile. Write 100–120 words.

....

....

....

....

....

....

....

....

....

....

Practice test paper

 Paper 1: Reading and usage (50 minutes)

Part 1

Questions 1 – 10

Read the text below, and for each number, circle the correct word on the next page.

"When you wish upon a star . . ."

Walt Disney and his brother Roy started 'Walt Disney', __(0)__ became one of the most __(1)__ companies in the world. Disney created characters such __(2)__ Mickey Mouse and Donald Duck and also had the idea for Disneyland and Walt Disney World. He __(3)__ 22 Academy Awards for his cartoons and movies.

It __(4)__ easy to think that life had always been a __(5)__ success for Walt Disney but that was not the case. He once lost his job working __(6)__ a newspaper because his employer did not think he was creative enough, and his first company __(7)__ closed down. Disney had no money and did not know what to do so he went __(8)__ Hollywood. He continued to have failures __(9)__ his films became successful. Walt never gave __(10)__ on his dreams – he never quit.

Example:

| 0 | (which) | who | they | can | [1] |

1	best	hated	famous	poorest	[1]
2	of	as	an	at	[1]
3	lost	won	had	is	[1]
4	will	is	would	can	[1]
5	small	tall	short	big	[1]
6	for	in	from	out	[1]
7	was	is	could	can	[1]
8	in	out	by	to	[1]
9	towards	until	at	in	[1]
10	out	up	in	on	[1]

[Turn over

Part 2

Questions 11 – 20

Complete the letter Neith is writing to her friend.
For questions **11 – 20**, write ONE word in each space.

Example: (0) _my_

Hello, **(0)** _my_ name is Neith. **(11)** .... live in the largest city and capital of Egypt,

Cairo. **(12)** .... is a lively city located **(13)** .... the river Nile. There is

(14) .... much to do here and everybody is very friendly and welcoming. **(15)** ....

must come and visit soon. **(16)** .... could go and visit the Pyramids of Giza, or

maybe you would like to go to the museum and visit the old city. I love swimming

(17) .... the Red Sea. I am always amazed **(18)** .... see the beautiful rainbow

coloured fish and other creatures that live in the sea. You are welcome anytime; the weather

is sunny most of the year. Summer is hot and lasts **(19)** .... May **(20)** ....

October and winter is very mild and starts in November and ends in April.

[Total: 10 marks]

Part 3

Questions 21 – 25

Complete the conversation between a mother and her son.

What does Mum say to Dan?

For questions **21 – 25**, write the correct letter **A – H.**

Example:

Mum: What shall we do today?

Dan: **0** __C__

Mum: I was thinking we could go to the cinema.

Dan: **21** .... [1]

Mum: Would you like to see a film in the afternoon and then eat?

Dan: **22** .... [1]

Mum: Are you hungry now?

Dan: **23** .... [1]

Mum: Shall we try the new Spanish restaurant?

Dan: **24** .... [1]

Mum: Have you heard it has good food?

Dan: **25** .... [1]

Mum: That's our plan then. We'll go to eat now and watch the new film afterwards.

A When does the film start?

B Yes, my friend Alexis went yesterday and really liked it.

C I don't know.

D I would prefer to go the Italian restaurant next door.

E I would like to eat first.

F That's a good idea. There's a new film I'd like to see.

G Yes, I'm really hungry.

H It looks like it might rain.

[Turn over

Part 4

Questions 26 – 35

Look at the text in each question.
What does it say?
Circle the correct letter **A**, **B** or **C**.

Example:

0

Mum,
I will be late home tonight
as I forgot to tell you that
I have a football match
after school. It may finish
early but if it doesn't I
should be back by 5 o'clock.

Love
Ben

A Ben will be home at 5 o'clock tonight.

Ⓑ Ben may be home before 5 o'clock tonight if the football match finishes early.

C Ben will be home later than 5 o'clock if the football match finishes early.

26

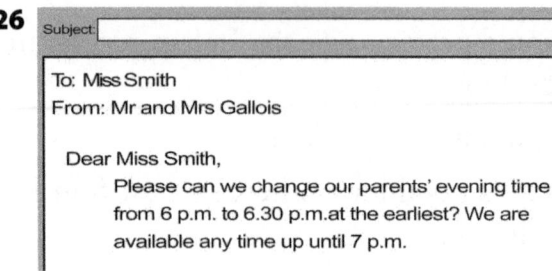

Subject:

To: Miss Smith
From: Mr and Mrs Gallois

Dear Miss Smith,
    Please can we change our parents' evening time from 6 p.m. to 6.30 p.m. at the earliest? We are available any time up until 7 p.m.

Mr and Mrs Gallois need to change their parents' evening appointment

A from 6 p.m. to any time between 6.30 p.m. and 7 p.m.

B from 6.30 p.m. to 6.00 p.m.

C from 6 p.m. to any time before. [1]

27

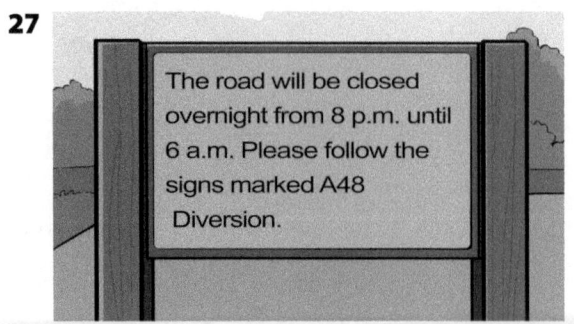

The road will be closed overnight from 8 p.m. until 6 a.m. Please follow the signs marked A48 Diversion.

A You can drive on the road tomorrow from 6 a.m.

B You cannot drive on the road from 6 a.m. tomorrow.

C You can drive on the road overnight. [1]

28

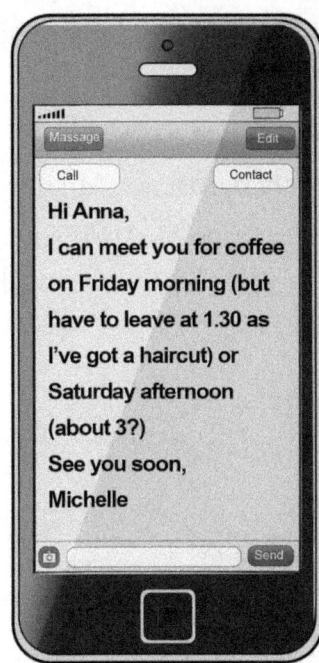

A Michelle can meet in the morning before her haircut on Saturday.

B Michelle can meet in the morning before her haircut on Friday.

C Michelle can meet in the morning after her haircut on Friday. [1]

29

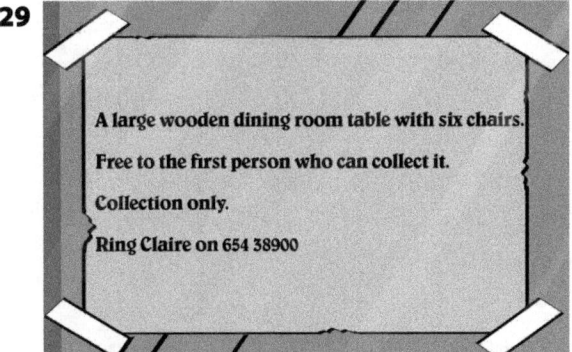

You ring Clare to

A discuss the price of the dining room table.

B give her directions to your house.

C arrange collecting the dining room table. [1]

30

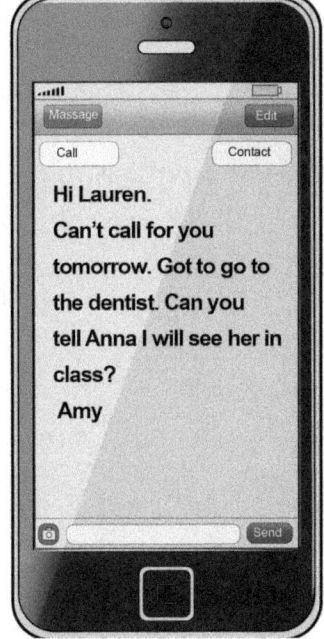

Amy has sent a text message to say

A she is not going to school tomorrow.

B she is going to the dentist and will not call for Anna.

C she can't call for Lauren as she's going to the dentist. [1]

[Turn over

31

Summer is coming

Buy one pair of sandals and get the second pair for half price

From 21 April until 28 April

Order online with code PAIR

To get the second pair of sandals half price, you have to

A buy three pairs of sandals on 21 April.

B buy two pairs of sandals before 21 April.

C buy one pair of sandals from 21 April to 28 April. [1]

32

Chloe, ring Lisa – your ballet lesson time needs to be changed (and remember to bring the ballet shoes for Lucy tonight).

Ella

Chloe needs to contact Lisa

A about the ballet shoes.

B to change the time of her lesson.

C about Ella. [1]

33

Subject:

Dear Parents,

Due to the snow, we are closing school early today. Please make arrangements for your children to be picked up at 2 p.m.

Many thanks, Mrs Granger

The email is sent to inform parents

A the school will be closed all week.

B to collect their children at 2 p.m. as the school is closing.

C the school will close if it starts to snow at 2 p.m. [1]

34

Swimming lessons
Beginners to advanced
Monday to Friday 5-6 p.m.
All welcome
For details ask at reception

A Lessons are for all swimmers every weekday, Monday to Friday, 5 p.m. until 6 p.m.

B Lessons are for beginner swimmers every weekday, Monday to Friday, 5 p.m. until 6 p.m.

C Lessons are for all swimmers every weekend. [1]

35

Dear Mr Wilson,

I am pleased to inform you that we would like to offer you the post of science teacher at The Success School starting 1 September. Please complete the attached form and return it to us by 2 July.

Yours sincerely,
Ms Demetriades

A The letter offers Mr Wilson a job as a science teacher.

B The letter asks Mr Wilson to come for a meeting.

C The letter says Mr Wilson has not been offered the job. [1]

[Turn over

Part 5

Questions 36 – 40

The people below all want to choose an after school club to join.

On the opposite page there are descriptions of eight different after school clubs offered at their school.

Decide which club would be the most suitable for the following people.

For questions **36 – 40**, write the correct letter (**A – H**) in the box.

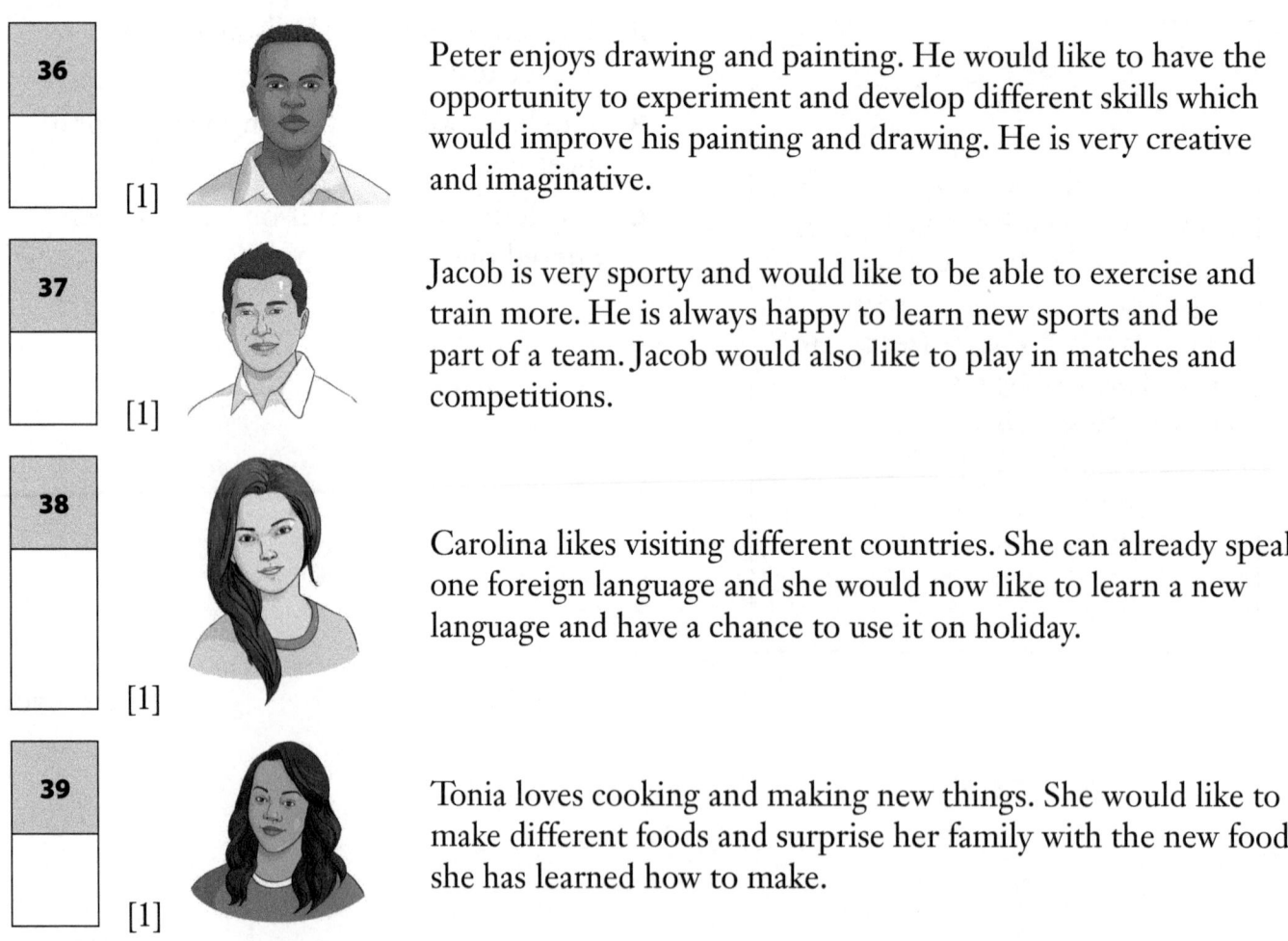

| 36 | [1] | | Peter enjoys drawing and painting. He would like to have the opportunity to experiment and develop different skills which would improve his painting and drawing. He is very creative and imaginative. |

| 37 | [1] | | Jacob is very sporty and would like to be able to exercise and train more. He is always happy to learn new sports and be part of a team. Jacob would also like to play in matches and competitions. |

| 38 | [1] | | Carolina likes visiting different countries. She can already speak one foreign language and she would now like to learn a new language and have a chance to use it on holiday. |

| 39 | [1] | | Tonia loves cooking and making new things. She would like to make different foods and surprise her family with the new food she has learned how to make. |

| 40 | [1] | | Danny enjoys spending his spare time outside and recently his family started a vegetable garden. Danny would like to know what to grow and when to plant it. |

A selection of after school clubs available

A Italian for beginners:
Wednesday 3.30 p.m. – 5 p.m.

Learn how to communicate in Italian, from an Italian. You will learn to speak, read and write basic Italian. Start now and be ready to have a full conversation on holiday in Italy next year.

B Vegetable gardening:
Tuesday 3 p.m. – 4.30 p.m.

We will be looking at ways of growing food for you and your family. Learn what vegetables grow the best here and how to care for them. We will practise our skills by designing, planting and taking care of the school's vegetable garden.

C Chess:
Friday 3.30 p.m. – 5 p.m.

Do you like to play chess? Maybe you have never played but you want to learn how. Join our club to learn the rules of chess or improve your current technique. You can even experience competition when you are ready!

D Ceramics and pottery:
Thursday 3 p.m. – 4.30 p.m.

Bring out your creative side and design ceramics and pottery. We design and make everything from cups to plates and afterwards you can decorate them in whichever way you wish. Combine this club with your painting and drawing classes to practise your skills.

E Five-a-side football:
Friday 3 p.m. – 5.30 p.m.

We meet every Friday to train and play a game of five-a-side football. Meet new people, keep fit and improve your game. I have been a football trainer for 10 years and before that I played professional football for a number of teams.

F Photography:
Monday 3 p.m. – 4.30 p.m.

An introduction to the world of photography. You will find out about light, darkness and how to make people feel comfortable while having their photographs taken. Come and learn how to take the perfect picture.

G Public speaking:
Tuesday 3 p.m. – 4.30 p.m.

We will look at how to prepare for giving a speech in public. Body language, voice control and the art of making a great speech will all be explored. A perfect way to prepare for a big event and become a more confident public speaker.

H Chinese cooking:
Monday 3 p.m. – 4.30 p.m.

Learn how to prepare and cook food using Chinese recipes. I am a trained chef and have worked as head chef in a Chinese restaurant for 15 years. I know all the inside secrets and will help you cook delicious Chinese food for your friends and family.

[Turn over

Part 6

Questions 41 – 45

Read the text and questions below.

For each question, circle the correct letter **A, B, C** or **D**.

Life in international schools

My name is Bernadette and I have had a very different childhood compared with my friends back home in Budapest, Hungary. My parents move countries every two to five years because their work takes them to different parts of the world.

I think I am very lucky. I have lived in three different countries and I am only 14 years old. I lived in Greece for three years, Italy for five years and now I'm in an international school in Singapore. I have learned so much about the world and I have made so many great friends that I'm not sure I can imagine going to the same school in my home country every day. My parents and I go back to Hungary every holiday and I see all my friends and family at least four times a year, so I still feel connected to my culture and language.

I love meeting people from all over the world, learning new languages and visiting new places. I like the fact that when people ask me where I'm from, I really feel that I am part of four different countries. Each country has made me who I am today. The worst part is having to say 'goodbye', but these days we can talk with everybody through social media – it's not like years ago when there were only phones and letters.

Speaking three different languages has certainly made me more confident and allowed me to learn new things about different cultures. After all, it is only really when you speak a language that you understand more about the culture of the country. International schools have given me great opportunities and skills. I am looking forward to the future and I wonder where I will be in two years' time.

41 What is the purpose of this text?
  A to give Bernadette's opinion of going to an international school
  B to persuade people to go to an international school
  C to give information about international schools
  D to warn people not to go to international schools   [1]

42 Why does Bernadette attend an international school?

   A She wanted to learn new languages.

   B She moves country every few years because of her parents' work.

   C She thinks it is a good way to meet people.

   D She wants to travel more.   [1]

43 Why does Bernadette consider herself very 'lucky'?

   A She has great parents.

   B She has a lovely family.

   C She has lived in three different countries.

   D She has lots of friends.   [1]

44 What does Bernadette love about being in an international school?

   A being with people from all over the world, learning new languages and visiting new places

   B being able to travel and still visit her home country

   C studying different subjects

   D being able to talk on social media   [1]

45 Which text message would the writer send to her friend who is moving to an international school in a new country?

A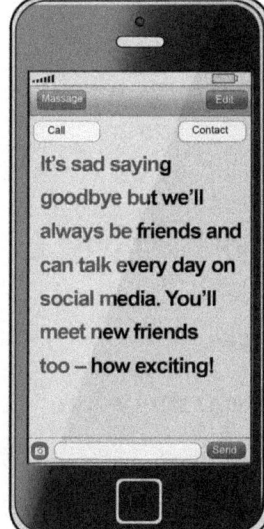

It's sad saying goodbye but we'll always be friends and can talk every day on social media. You'll meet new friends too – how exciting!

B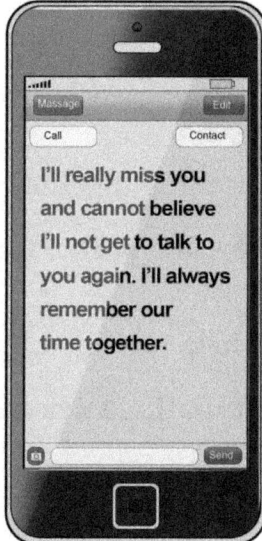

I'll really miss you and cannot believe I'll not get to talk to you again. I'll always remember our time together.

C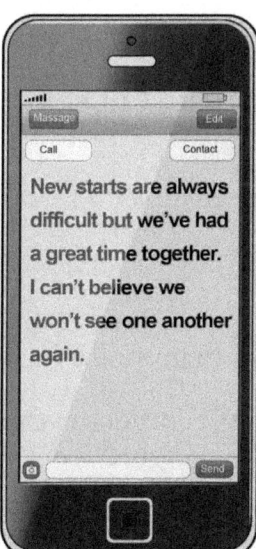

New starts are always difficult but we've had a great time together. I can't believe we won't see one another again.

D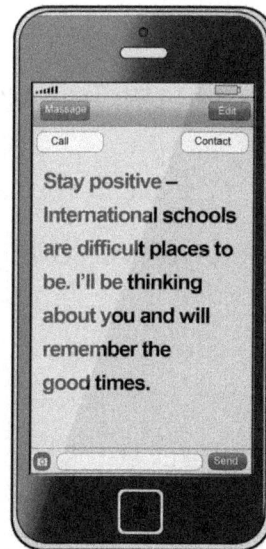

Stay positive – International schools are difficult places to be. I'll be thinking about you and will remember the good times.

Paper 2: Writing (50 minutes)

Part 1

Questions 1 – 5

For questions **1 – 5**, complete the second sentence so that it means the same as the first sentence.

Use no more than three words.

Write only the missing words.

Example:

0 Today I wrote an essay about the people who live on my street.

Today I have written an essay about the people who live on my street.

---

1 My best friend lives in the house with a red door.

The house with the red door is the one .... my best friend lives.   [1]

2 Her house is the same as ours but the garden is larger.

Our houses are the same but she .... larger garden.   [1]

3 We are in the same class at school and do everything together.

I do everything .... her as we are in the same class at school.   [1]

4 She is better at maths than me so I ask her to help me when I get stuck.

... she is better than me at maths, I ask her to help me when I get stuck.   [1]

5 In return I help her with her essay writing.

In return I help her .... write her essays.   [1]

Part 2

Question 6

Jamal invited you to his party. You accepted the invitation but have learned that you are no longer free to go. The party is tomorrow.

Write an email to Jamal.

Tell Jamal:

- how sorry you are
- why you can no longer go
- what your hopes are for his party.

Write 35 – 45 words.

Write the email below.

....

....

....

....

....

....

....

....

[10]

[Turn over

Part 3

Question 7

You see an essay-writing competition in a magazine and decide to enter. Essays must be written on the following subject:

Write a description of yourself, where you will be living, and what you hope you will be doing in ten years' time.

Write your essay in **100 – 120 words** in an appropriate style below.

....

....

....

....

....

....

....

....

....

....

....

[20]

Paper 3: Listening (45 minutes)

Part 1

Questions 1 – 5

For each question, there are three pictures and a short recording.
Choose the correct picture and circle the letter **A**, **B** or **C** below it.

Example: Which of Sam's activities has been cancelled this week?

A   B   Ⓒ

---

1 What did Scott leave behind at home today?

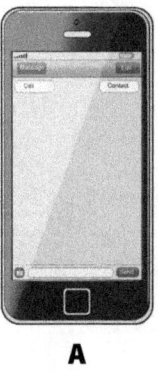 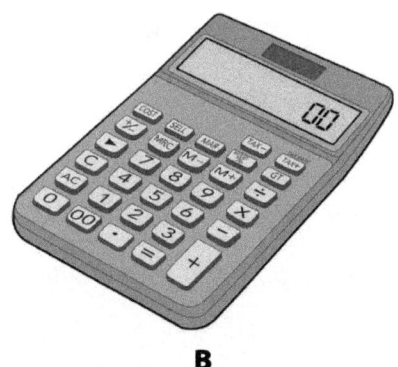 

A   B   C

[1]

2 How much will each cinema ticket cost this evening?

A   B   C

[1]

[Turn over

3 What will Max buy his teacher for helping him?

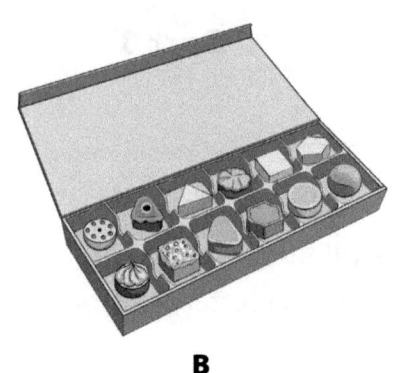

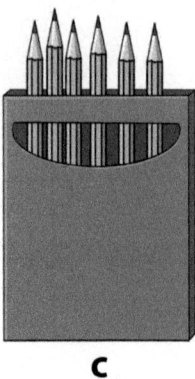

A   B   C

[1]

4 What does Harry have to do before going to school this morning?

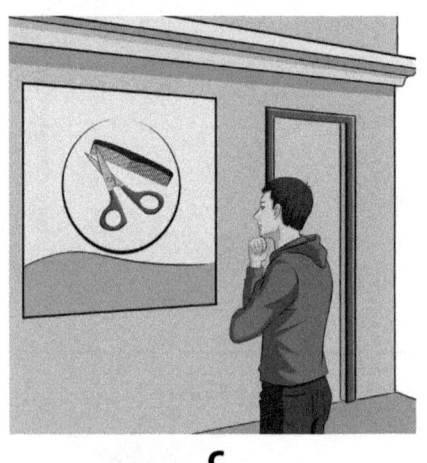

A   B   C

[1]

5 Which museum will the girls visit today?

A   B   C

[1]

Part 2

Questions 6 – 10

For each question, there are three pictures and a short recording.

Choose the correct picture and circle the letter **A**, **B** or **C** below it.

---

6 When will the student go to the lesson?

     A   **B**   **C**

[1]

7 What topic will the class be studying next in science?

     A   **B**   **C**

[1]

8 Which dress does Margo decide to buy?

     A   **B**   **C**

[1]

[Turn over

9 Where is Jane's book?

A

B

C

[1]

10 Where are the family going on their next holiday?

A

B

C

[1]

Part 3

Questions 11 – 15

You will hear people talking in five different situations.
For each question, circle the correct answer **A**, **B** or **C**.

---

11 You hear a girl talking about her party.

What kind of party did she have?

A a bead party

B a clay modelling party

C a rock-climbing party   [1]

12 You hear a teacher telling her class about a school trip they are going on.

Where is the class going?

A the seaside

B the local park

C the funfair   [1]

13 You hear an old man talk about something that happened when he was younger.

What event is he remembering in his talk?

A the first time he drove a car

B the first time he went into space

C the first time he went in an aeroplane   [1]

14 You hear part of a talk given by a museum guide.

Which room is the newest room in the museum?

A the Planets Room

B the Oxygen Room

C the Underwater Room   [1]

15 You hear a tour guide talking about the Dinosaur Park you are visiting.

Which part of the Dinosaur Park is closed at the moment?

A the Dinosaur Trail

B the Moving Dinosaur Exhibition

C the Dinosaur Play Park   [1]

[Turn over

Part 4

Questions 16 – 20

You will hear an interview with a man called Dominic Frost, who is talking about his work as a sculptor.

For each question, circle the correct answer **A**, **B** or **C**.

---

16 Who introduced Dominic to sculpture?

   A his father

   B his teacher

   C his sister   [1]

17 What does Dominic enjoy most about his job?

   A the hours

   B the money

   C the freedom   [1]

18 When does Dominic get his ideas for his sculptures?

   A when he walks in the park

   B when he reads magazines

   C when he goes to the library   [1]

19 How does Dominic improve his work?

   A he asks his old teacher

   B he asks his wife for a second opinion

   C his work never needs improvement   [1]

20 What will be the subject of Dominic's next sculpture?

   A a boy sitting on a bench

   B a boy standing on a beach

   C a boy painting a boat   [1]

Part 5

Questions 21 – 25

You will hear a guide telling some tourists about some safety
rules at an outdoor adventure park.

For each question, fill in the missing information in the numbered space.

TREE WALK ADVENTURE PARK

Safety
- Always wear your helmet
- Make sure your safety **(21)** .... is always attached
- Let the person in front of you finish the zip wire before you start

Cost
- £10 per day, including instruction and **(22)** .... equipment
- £8 per day if you have visited in the last **(23)** .... months

What else you can do
- The café
  - make sure you try one of our **(24)** .... meals
- The shop
  - spend some of your pocket money on small souvenirs
  - get a special **(25)** .... to get your discount next time you come

[Total: 5 marks]

[Turn over

Part 6

Questions 26 – 30

You will hear an interview with Aisha Cole, who worked as a teacher before she became a pilot. For each question, circle the correct answer **A**, **B** or **C**.

---

26 Aisha says she left teaching because

  A she wanted to learn a new skill.

  B she wanted to travel around the whole world.

  C she had always wanted to become a pilot.   [1]

27 How did Aisha feel after she started the pilot's course?

  A She was very excited because she had wanted to do it for a long time.

  B She was a little nervous about whether she had made the right choice.

  C She was relaxed because she knew she was doing the right thing for her.   [1]

28 What did Aisha almost forget to do on her first professional flight?

  A She nearly forgot to talk to the passengers before take-off.

  B She nearly forgot to tell her co-pilot where they were flying to.

  C She nearly forgot to order herself some lunch for the journey.   [1]

29 How does Aisha say her life has changed now she is a pilot?

  A She gets recognised by people who live in the same town as her.

  B She often meets passengers who she used to teach.

  C She goes to work happier than ever before.   [1]

30 What plans does Aisha have for the future?

  A She would like to learn how to fly a helicopter.

  B She would like to pilot longer distance flights to Australia.

  C She would like to be the first female chief pilot of the airline.   [1]